The King of Greenpoint

Geoffrey Cobb

ISBN-13: 978-1537442082
ISBN-10: 1537442082

Peter J. McGuinness

The Amazing Story of Greenpoint's Most Colorful Character

Contents

Introduction

It was New Year's Eve and I had just completed the draft of this book. Someone came to me with exciting news, explaining that he met a local woman who had known Pete McGuinness. I met the 88-year-old woman and asked about meeting McGuinness.

She told me her father worked as a cook on a tugboat to support the family, but the depression killed his work and the family was so broke that they could not buy food. The hungry family, in desperation, went to McGuinness' club at 119 Norman Avenue where the woman's mother explained the family's plight to McGuinness. Hearing the family was hungry, he reached into his pocket and gave the woman, then a twelve-year-old girl, a dollar so that the family could buy food. I looked in the elderly woman's eyes, but they were far away, glazed over in memory and then a smile passed over her face. She said softly to me, "He was a very good man."

The affluence in Greenpoint today seems light years away from McGuinness time during the Depression. The area has gentrified. The working class from whom Pete arose has largely been forced out by the high rents. Ritzy boutiques, nail salons and trendy eateries have replaced the mom and pop shops that once characterized the area.

Some might question the value in telling a story of the man who personified Greenpoint's almost vanished working class. They would argue that the story of New York's last ward boss who looked after his constituency of factory workers and longshoreman is no longer relevant. Luxury high-rise towers are fast replacing the factories of McGuinness day. These factories and other signs of McGuinness and his world are rapidly disappearing.

The McGuinness' story is relevant, though, for a number of reasons. We live in an age of extreme cynicism about government and politicians, but McGuinness who never went to high school, nevertheless made government work for the people. A beloved figure, McGuinness ran Greenpoint as a benevolent despot for almost thirty years until his death in 1948.

There are still a number of landmarks that bear witness to his legislative abilities. He got Greenpoint the subway, three parks, the bridge at the end of the Boulevard named in his honor, The McCarren Park Pool and other civic improvements, but people did not love him for these accomplishments. Greenpointers loved him not only because he was colorful and flamboyant, but also because he cared about them and their problems. They adored him because his humor shone through the darkest moments of the Great Depression. He was a larger-than-life character who so embodied the place that it was hard to think about Greenpoint without thinking about him and vice versa.

Most of all the McGuinness' story is fun. He was a unique, funny loveable character who loved Greenpoint as much as it loved him. The *Greenpoint Star* referred to him as "The Spirit of Greenpoint." Writing about McGuinness was fun and I hope that you enjoy reading it as much as I enjoyed putting it on paper. The first three chapters mix imagination and historical research, but all the characters and all the events are real.

Peter McGuinness Greenpoint Map

A) McGuinness' birthplace – 132 Eagle Street

B) Orr' Lumber Yard – Pete's Place of Employment Green Street and West

C) J. J. Byrne Bridge – Acquired by McGuinness in 1927

D) John McQuade Club – Corner of Manhattan and Meserole Avenues

E) Second home of Greenpoint People's Regular Democratic Club 119 Norman Avenue

F) Original home of Greenpoint People's Regular Democratic Club – Meserole Avenue, just down from the 94th Precinct

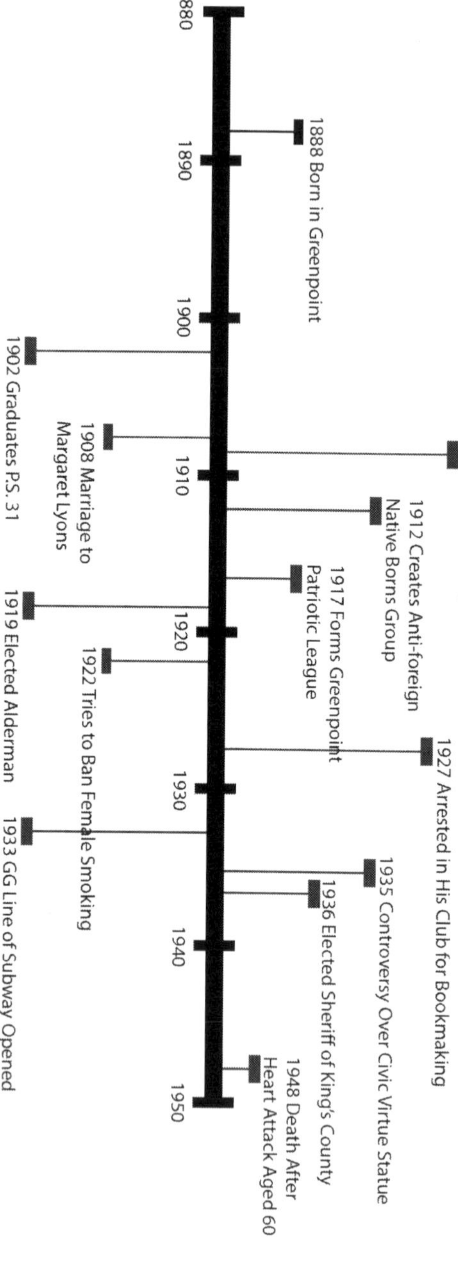
Peter McGuinness Timeline
1880
1890
1900
1910
1920
1930
1940
1950
1888 Born in Greenpoint
1902 Graduates P.S. 31
1908 Marriage to Margaret Lyons
1909 Works as Longshoreman
1912 Creates Anti-foreign Native Borns Group
1917 Forms Greenpoint Patriotic League
1919 Elected Alderman
1922 Tries to Ban Female Smoking
1927 Arrested in His Club for Bookmaking
1933 GG Line of Subway Opened
1935 Controversy Over Civic Virtue Statue
1936 Elected Sheriff of King's County
1948 Death After Heart Attack Aged 60

Chapter One: Manhattan Avenue March 10, 1927

Let's imagine an unusually mild mid-March Saturday afternoon in Greenpoint, Brooklyn. The breeze still had a slight chill, but the sun warmed the skies, bathing the area in bright sunlight. Families were taking advantage of the sun to shop in the many small shops that lined Manhattan Avenue, the main street of the neighborhood. Three small boys from one of these families dallied in front of the chocolates in the candy store window, but a threatening look from their mother made them move promptly, despite their great reluctance. A keener eye would have noticed the modest clothes of the family. The father wore work-faded pants and a simple cotton shirt; the mother wore a simple cotton dress and a worn woolen sweater. The threadbare look of some of the children's clothes betrayed the fact that they were hand-me-downs, yet they were a happy family, enjoying the afternoon, typical of the many working-class Greenpoint people out on the avenue.

Assistant District Attorney James Cuff bounded out from the James McQuade political club on the corner of Meserole and Manhattan Avenues, clearly different in appearance than the working-class families he rushed by. Quite well dressed in his gray, well-tailored woolen suit and polished leather shoes, Cuff's fine clothes set him apart from his modestly dressed blue-collar neighbors on the avenue.

Cuff, enjoying the sun, walked briskly, while whistling an Irish tune. He radiated self-satisfaction and contentment, but as he looked down the avenue, suddenly his eye caught sight of a figure and his mood instantaneously darkened. His lip curled in contempt and his smile disappeared. He spat out, "Oh God it is that big fat buffoon McGuinness holding court right out here on the street like some Tammany politician of the nineties. What a disgrace."

Cuff, though, decided to stay a while. Perhaps the loudmouth would say something that Registrar McQuade could use as ammunition. Scornfully turning to watch McGuinness, he said to himself, "I cannot believe that the people of Greenpoint are such rubes that they would actually vote for a clown like this. Imagine a lumber handler with only an eighth-grade education not only as alderman, but also as district leader." Cuff still could not believe that the people had chosen this fool over Registrar McQuade, a far more educated and well-spoken man than this stevedore low-life. He sneered and thought, "And he even calls himself the King of Greenpoint. He'll get his soon enough." Then the D.A. began to watch the street theater scene that unfolded every time McGuinness held court on the avenue.

McGuinness regularly presided on the corner of Manhattan Avenue and Norman Avenue on fine Saturdays like today, just as the Tammany Hall political chieftains of old New York had done. He propped his large body against a light pole, greeting the pedestrians by their first names, mingling with his constituents and laughing regularly. People expressed joy upon seeing the "Boss of Greenpoint," and a large crowd had quickly formed around him. As other people across the street caught sight of him, they dodged the trolley, crossing the avenue to share a few words with "The McGuinness."

Peter stood out in any crowd. A big, tough, happy, red-faced Irishman, he was a powerful man who stood over six feet, and easily weighing two hundred and seventy pounds with a barrel chest and large muscular arms. Years of grueling physical work moving mountains of lumber had also developed a hard, agile body, which has taken on weight without becoming slovenly. McGuinness did not look fat. He looked beefy, powerful, massive and stately. He carried his body and his head erect. His walk was slow, lordly, and rather ponderously graceful.

Boss McGuinness somehow seemed out of place in 1927. He was an anachronism, and every aspect of his appearance seemed to harken back thirty years before to the gay nineties. Everything about McGuinness resembled a nineteenth century Irish ward boss. He often wore a straw hat that had been out of fashion for decades. Unlike the politicians of the era to which he belonged, he was anything but flashy in dress. He wore a gray tweed suit, a white shirt, a quietly patterned blue tie, black high-top shoes and white cotton socks.

The alderman had a massive head, clear blue eyes, and a complexion a shade or two off ripe tomato. His hair was pure white, yet still plentiful. He parted it neatly in the middle and scalloped it daintily over his forehead in the roach style affected by bartenders fifty years earlier. His nose and chin were huge, granitic affairs that jutted far out from their moorings in the face and then tilted sharply upward. The face, all in all, seemed the work of a sculptor of large and noble intentions, but of either imprecise, poor or cunningly ambiguous execution.

Cuff, though twenty yards away, could hear him clearly, so loud was the alderman's voice. McGuinness' face was a complete contrast to Cuff's sneer. McGuinness radiated joy and his eyes sparkled as he boomed out gusty big helloes. He enjoyed giving people the big hello, just as he enjoyed everything else about politics. He liked making speeches; marching in parades; attending weddings, christenings, confirmations, and funerals, and running Kiddies-Day outings. The joy, enthusiasm and humor he radiated attracted people. He knew everyone on the street very and greeted the men as "My old pal" or as "My old Pork chop," inquiring about their sisters, brothers, aunts and uncles. McGuinness clearly not only knew his constituents, but also their entire families. The men were greeted with a powerful McGuinness backslap and a wrenching handshake, the ladies with a warm, friendly smile. The huge hands that greeted them were the hands of a longshoreman-rough and calloused from years of moving rough boards each day.

His only ring was a solid gold one, set with a garnet, which was given to him eighteen years earlier by his wife, Margaret, a handsome woman of proportions almost as large as his own. He spoke of her, as a rule, as "the old champeen." The members of McGuinness' club once raised a thousand dollars and bought him a ring, but although they had bought the largest band the jeweler stocked, it would not fit on any of his fingers, which were as big around as pick handles. "Bless us, but it don't even go on the pinky," he said in his speech at the presentation ceremony, trying to make the best of an awkward situation. The possession of it proved an embarrassment to him. He felt it would make him a fancy dude, something he loathed.

Suddenly, a red-nosed, freckled, blue-eyed, Irish-looking man called out, "'Bejesus, there's Petey McGuinness in the gutter. Hello, Petey me boy, what are you doing here today?" Pete replied, "Oh, I'm fine, thank you, Mr. Flaherty. I was just standing in the gutter here because it's so nice and sunny. How are you today and how is dear Mrs. Flaherty?" Then McGuinness asked him about "woik" in the Navy Yard and about the chance of jobs for some of the local boys.

A family with six small kids approached McGuinness and a tiny girl in a white cotton dress ran ahead of her family, calling for uncle Petey, and grabbed his arm with a look of rapture on her tiny face. McGuinness broke off the conversation with the man he was talking to, and with a look of joy equal to hers, he lifted her clean off the ground, holding her high aloft, much to the child's sheer delight. "Mary Anne, You're a big 'goil' now," he said, and after a few seconds in the air he put her down on the ground. Then he reached into the cavernous pocket of his large grey alpaca overcoat, pulling out a wad of wrapped chocolates, which he gave to her and all the other children. He liked children, which they sensed, and returned their affection through warm smiles and laughter.

Suddenly, the mood changed. A large, powerful man dressed in overalls and a lumber handler's apron approached Pete menacingly, and the smile and joy in McGuinness' eyes changed instantaneously. Pete scowled and pulled his massive fists out of his coat. The crowd, sensing imminent conflict, immediately backed off, forming a circle. Pete crouched and raised his fists to eye level as his would-be opponent took the same pose. McGuinness clenched his immense fists, crouched forward and started jabbing sharply at his antagonist. "You louse-bastard, you," he said. "Who you think you're talking to? Huh?" The two men circled each other, looking to throw blows. Tension filled the air and the crowd looked apprehensive, but suddenly, both men burst out laughing, dropped their fists and gave each other a bear hug. "How ya doin' Petey," said the man. "Duffy, me old pal from the lumber yard. It's great to see you," exclaimed Pete.

There were smiles of relief all around and Duffy told the crowd how he had boxed against Pete as a teenager right here on Manhattan Avenue in the Standard Athletic club. He spoke about Pete's quick hands and ability to take a punch. He told the crowd of Pete's granite jaw and hard jabs, while also relating how Pete had won thirteen fights and drew two as an amateur, but suddenly he was interrupted by a pimply faced teenager who asked, "So if he was so good in the ring, why's he a politician and not a boxer?“ Duffy with mild indignation said, “Listen kid, if Pete’d wanted to be a boxer he coulda been, but Petey didn’t like hurting people who didn’t deserve it. Petey just didn’t like the ring. He was born to look after us here in Greenpernt,” and when the alderman heard this he smiled and nodded his head in agreement.

Duffy explained to the circle of people on the sidewalk that Pete was not just good in the ring, but in the lumberyard too. He reckoned that Pete was the toughest dock walloper he had ever seen and that he could not only lick anyone in a punch up on the docks from here to Irishtown, but he could also move more lumber than the best of them. They shook hands warmly and Pete’s old sparring partner moved on.

Over the next three hours or so, dozens of people approached Pete, many with some intimate secret to share. Pete often bent down to let them whisper in his ear. Once Pete’s countenance grew serious and he responded in a low voice to a man, “Come to my club this week. Don’t you worry, old Petey will be able to work it out.” He also told a few others to come and see him at his club.

An imaginative person could easily have envisioned Pete not as some Greenpoint ward boss, but as a beefy ancient Roman senator bestowing patronage on the plebeians, so paternal and regal was his bearing. Laughing and glad-handing, Pete was definitely in his element and it seemed that nothing could break the people's love for McGuinness, but appearances can be deceiving.

McGuinness was the last ward boss in the city who practiced this old Tammany Hall custom of greeting the voters on the street corner. Some educated voters looked down on it as a relic of New York's dark Tammany past, and it may have died out in other parts of the city, but most Greenpointers still loved it. Tammany Hall corruption, though, would enter McGuinness' life in a way he could never have imagined.

On this afternoon, Pete seemed to be at the peak of his popularity. No one could have guessed that, in a few days, an event would occur right in his very own club that would cast a long, dark shadow on McGuinness' rule, threatening his reign as "King of Greenpoint."

Chapter Two: The Greenpoint People's Regular Democratic Club

The essence of Pete's popularity and power was in performing "contracts" for his constituents. These contracts involved solving problems and were signatures of machine politics and political clubhouses and a defining feature of New York's political culture for generations. Years later, a reporter asked Pete about the nature of these contracts. Considering these contracts as something sacred, he refused to divulge their details, but explained, "I never talk about me people's troubles, but you know how it is. You're walking along the street, and somebody you don't even know bunks into you. So you give him the back of your hand, and he comes back for more. One of that kind, you know. You give him another, and he's back again. You belt him good, and then some goddam patrolman busts in and takes the two of yez down to the station. He don't know who started it, so it's drunk and disorderly, the two of yez. What the hell are you going to do? All the nerves in your body are jumping. Your pulse is throbbing hard. You're cold all over. You're thinking you ain't got a friend in the world. Then, it comes to you. 'I'll call Peter McGuinness, you say to yourself. 'He'll get me out of this."

The mundane activities in the clubhouse seemed so unremarkable that no one could have imagined that in a few hours this sleepy run down old Ambassador Hotel, which housed McGuinness' club, would witness a scene that would make citywide headlines and threaten to depose the "King of Greenpoint."

The hotel had been home to a Masonic lodge once, but the Masons had long since left Greenpoint and the building was an architectural anachronism. When describing the old building, the words drab and dingy immediately sprung to mind. The weathered old brownstone building stood on the corner of Meserole and Manhattan Avenue, only two doors down from the precinct and just across the street from the club of Pete's archrival, Registrar James McQuade. A high granite staircase led to the doors on the first floor. There was peeling paint on the wooden doors that had surely seen better days long ago. The four-story building had an elevator, but nobody could remember when it actually worked. A tired iron staircase led to the second and third floors where McGuinness made his contracts.

The contracts were extremely varied. They could include getting a judge to pardon a ticket, cajoling a landlord or solving domestic disputes. Pete took them extremely seriously, for he measured himself as an effective politician by his performance in completing his end of these contracts. Almost every night of the year Pete arrived in his club at eight o'clock to meet his constituents and solve their problems.

No one was turned away and many a troubled Greenpointer ended up in Pete's club. A visitor entered a large waiting room for McGuinness' constituents. The walls of the waiting room were dingy and smelled heavily of cigar and cigarette smoke. On the walls of the large, gloomy room there were blown-up, tinted portraits of McGuinness with his arms around Jimmy Walker, a bust of Thomas Jefferson, a faded pennant bearing the name and likeness of Governor Franklin D. Roosevelt, and a huge picture of McGuinness as a brawny young dock walloper. The room was sparsely furnished and what was there was old and worn. Constituents started arriving shortly after six and waited their turn in straight-backed chairs. By the time that Pete arrived there were a dozen or so careworn faces, fidgeting and waiting to see the boss.

McGuinness arrived, greeting all the guests with a booming hello and his signature, wrenching handshake. He took off his coat, placing it on a rickety old coat stand in the corner of the room and entering his office, which contained a large cast iron standing safe, McGuinness' big weathered old desk and a table for his stenographer. Nearby were two more tables for McGuinness' assistants.

McGuinness was in his club almost every night of the year, usually staying there until twelve thirty or one. He normally saw anywhere from a dozen to a hundred people before ten o'clock. Fulfilling the contracts had not only won Pete votes, but it had also earned him heartfelt gratitude. Some of his constituents were so grateful that they offered McGuinness money, but the offer of money could change Pete from affable uncle to stern father figure. If the person persisted, Pete told him in no uncertain terms that he would accept no money and if he or she did not stop, the person was asked immediately to leave the premises.

Let's imagine a typical night of contracts. The procession of troubled souls started. The first to enter Pete's office was Mrs. O'Reilly, a widow and the owner of a boarding house near Orr's lumberyard, where Pete once worked. Three years ago her poodle nipped the leg of a neighbor, Mrs. O'Leary. Mrs. O' Reilly paid the doctor bills and the wound had long since healed, but the widow had just learned she was being sued by Mrs. O'Leary for three hundred dollars in damages—a huge amount of money to the widow. Pete patiently heard the widow's story and then he waived his arms and said gruffly, "It's a holdup.

Don't worry about it, but, don't give her a cent. Go Home, Mrs. O'Reilly, and don't fret about it any more."

Next into the office was a teenage girl of eighteen or nineteen, a pretty redhead with an air of mixed boredom and defiance. Her father, a night watchman in the Navy Yard, had seen Pete on the street yesterday and McGuinness told him to send the girl to the club. Learning her identity, Pete began a parley with the girl, whose face was a perfect study of contempt and disinterest. Pete learned that the girl's mother had died and that her was upset feared because he feared she was staying out late with a bad crowd, while ignoring her father's pleas. The young woman affected an air of studied detachment as she listened to McGuinness. Then suddenly, McGuinness began to speak about his own mother and his voice choked with emotion, while tears began to form in his eyes. He said, "Think of your dead mother and your father. You have only one parent left now and you had better obey him." McGuinness' raw emotions touched the girl and instantly her demeanor changed. The boredom vanished and the girl seemed genuinely moved. She promised him that she would respect her father's wishes and left.

Next into his office came Mrs. McGarragh, a plump brunette in her fifties, who began to tell the alderman that her husband has not been home for a week and that he was probably on the drink again. She was considering going to the police to have him arrested because she had heard that she could collect a pension as the wife of a jailed man. McGuinness suddenly became irritable and told his assistants to go to one of the local speakeasies and fetch Mr. McGarragh. He added angrily, "I do not care how drunk he is! Bring him right here now." He then snapped, "You have been listening to one of your evil neighbors. There is no such pension and if you are not careful you could end up in jail."

In the course of a few minutes there was a loud commotion at the door and a red-faced McGarragh was pushed into the office. He staggered towards Pete's desk, reeking of moonshine. When he saw his spouse a look of fear and dread swept over his face. Pete jumped up, grabbed him by his shirt and threw him roughly into a chair beside his wife. The alderman barked at the drunk, "You think you are tough; well I'm a lot tougher. You go home with your woman and you keep away from the booze." The chastised man sheepishly left with his spouse.

A steam of others kept filing into the office seeking redress. Pete made contracts to assuage threatening landlords and wrote letters to trolley companies and Brooklyn Union Gas trying to secure employment for men. There was a red-faced boy with his father who had stolen from a candy shop, but Pete had promised to talk to the judge in his case. The pedestrian nature of many of the contracts might have bored another man, but Pete seemed genuinely concerned, no matter how small the matter.

For Pete this was an ordinary night spent dispensing his brand of local justice, but the police were aware of criminal activities transpiring right inside his club and were determined to stop it. McGuinness had no idea that for weeks his club had been wiretapped and the police had been planning a raid that would soon make headlines.

Chapter Three: March 11, 1927 Police Headquarters

Inspector Lewis J. Valentine of the Police Department's feared Confidential Squad opened the People's Regular Democratic Club dossier on his desk and looked at the photograph of McGuinness. He despised politicians like McGuinness because they were guilty of allowing corruption and crime to fester. The thought of raiding McGuinness' club and arresting him delighted him. It was high time that rats like McGuinness were dragged out into the light and exposed.

Valentine had known McGuinness for years. The inspector had served as a cop on Greenpoint Avenue and he recalled McGuinness' campaign for alderman, laughing bitterly at McGuinness' claims to be, "as clean as a whistle." "What a joke!" he said to himself, as he thought about the gamblers and bootleggers with whom McGuinness associated.

If New York was a sewer, the inspector thought, it

was because of corrupt politicians like McGuinnness. He thought of the phony, burly alderman smiling and shaking hands on the street corner and it disgusted him. He hated most politicians, but he had an intense dislike for corrupt ward bosses like McGuinness who turned a blind eye to the rackets and gangsters destroying the city. For years Valentine had raged in angry silence, fuming at the ability of politicians like McGuinness to break the law and profit from it, but soon he would get his revenge.

The Kirwan brothers, known professional gamblers, had grown up on Eagle Street, just down from where McGuinness was born. McGuinness not only condoned the gambling that robbed families of rent and food money, but he even let the brothers use his own club for their poker games and track action. It disgusted him to think that honest beat cops could barely feed their families, while these gamblers lived the high life and paid no taxes, and no place had more gamblers, speakeasies and bootleggers than Greenpoint. For years, though, McGuinness had not only pretended these crimes did not exist, but he had even called for the disbanding of the Confidential Squad that fought bookmakers, bootleggers and other scum. The other boys on the squad also had a grudge against McGuinness and also relished the idea of getting some payback.

Valentine reflected on his long career on the force. He

was honest, just like his hard-working German-American father, a greengrocer who was poor, but never stole. Taking after his father, Valentine was never anything other than an honest cop, but his honesty had caused him a lot of grief. Born close-by in Williamsburg, he was the son of an Irish immigrant mother who worked in the family store alongside her husband and from whom he had inherited the Irish love of police work. He recalled his Irish-American mentor, Honest Dan Costigan, who had fought to rid the force of corrupt cops. Every Christmas the ward politicians made their annual pretentious gesture of giving gifts of food to the needy, while the rest of the year the poor starved. Costigan was truly generous. Although he was on a meager salary, he still gave a lot of his pay to the poor without the show that politicians put on when they helped the poor at Christmas. Of course, he was offered big bribes, which Costigan, a man of integrity, refused. Valentine admired him and followed in his footsteps.

The Becker scandal in 1912 changed everything. Becker was the kind of corrupt cop he hated and who gave the force a bad name. A lieutenant on Broadway in Manhattan, Becker banked $70,000 in two years as a partner in a gambling den on a salary of $90 a week. When his partner went to the District Attorney, complaining about excessive police skimming of profits, killers hired by Becker gunned him down in cold blood. The scandalous murder led Becker to the electric chair. The public demanded the resignation of the police commissioner, but again the politicians protected him.

The voters were so outraged that they voted the corrupt Tammany Hall mayor out of power and elected a reform administration under Johnny Puroy Mitchell who created the Confidential Squad to clean up police corruption. Mitchell chose Costigan to run the squad who appointed Valentine to it. Valentine quickly made a reputation for himself as a tough, honest detective, but the Confidential Squad aroused the ire of Tammany, which simply waited till the next election for payback. When the reform mayor was defeated in the next election, Tammany was back in power. The Confidential squad was disbanded and Valentine was sent packing. They laughed at him and told him to enjoy being stationed in Siberia. Valentine recalled raging in silent frustration during those long lonely nights, unable to fight the corruption he so despised.

He always burned with righteous indignation when he thought of how many corrupt cops of far lesser ability had gotten the promotions he deserved because of the influence of some "Rabbi," a connected politician like McGuinness who controlled police department promotions. Of course, there were kickbacks, but the worst thing was that there were hundreds of senior police officers beholden to these crooked politicians who turned a blind eye to rackets, just like the one in McGuinness' very own club.

Finally, the mayor appointed a new honest city police commissioner, John McLaughlin, who, from his first day in office, signaled his desire to root out graft by recreating the Confidential Squad. McLaughlin brazenly cut the ties with Tammany Hall. He reappointed Costigan to head the Confidential Squad with Valentine as Deputy Inspector.

The money of gamblers had purchased politicians, but McLaughlin changed everything. Suddenly, high-ranking cops owned by politicians were transferred. He was ridding the city of the rotten gamblers and the cheap politicians they bought. The gamblers had paid huge amounts of money to bribe cops, but now his squad had declared war against them.

He thought back on his years on the force. He became a New York policeman at age 21 in November 1903, and spent ten years walking a Flatbush beat. Valentine was now a twenty-four year-veteran of the force, but for years he had repeatedly been passed over for less-qualified men because he played by the rules and didn't take bribes. He passed the exam for sergeant with high marks, but others got the promotion, he merited. Part of the reason Valentine loathed McGuinness was because McGuinness was always looking to browbeat the commissioner into hiring, or promoting, his political friends, which infuriated Valentine.

He recalled his anger, which lasted many years, each time the list for new sergeants came out without his name there. The police were very poorly paid and the fact that he was married with a son to support only increased his anger at the corruption in promotions and the schemers who controlled it. Finally, On October 10, 1913, he was made sergeant. He later learned, much to his chagrin, that even his making sergeant was the result of the intervention of Congressman William Calder, a neighbor.

Valentine was proud of his reputation as a tough, butt-kicking cop. Some cops had given him the nickname “nightstick” because he was so skilled in using it to administer a beating. He thought back with great satisfaction on how the smirks of the punks he had arrested disappeared when he gave them the good beating they so thoroughly deserved. All these years later, he remained nostalgic about those simpler times when all a cop had to be was big and beefy, the best friend of everyone on the block, except the malefactor who needed his head cracked.

The police knew that raiding McGuinness’ club would cause a firestorm of protest and tried to avoid it by going to McGuinness’ boss, John McCooey, the Democratic leader of Brooklyn, telling him to warn McGuinness about the illegal gambling. McGuinness met with McCooey, but he brushed off the warning because the local Greenpoint police were totally loyal to him and would tip him off before any raid. Valentine laughed to himself because the police had an ingenious plan to sidestep the Greenpoint cops. Valentine and McLaughlin had planned the raid so carefully that McGuinness would never suspect it. In a few hours, Valentine laughed to himself, they would spring the trap and "Honest Pete" McGuinness would be exposed to the world. Valentine could hardly wait.

Chapter Four: The Raid – March 13, 1927

None of the hundred or so people in McGuinness' political club had any inkling that in a few minutes a scene would play out that would be headline news for all the major New York newspapers, but that would also be the focal point of a New York State commission investigating corruption. The Kirwan brothers were holding a poker game and taking bets on the horses as usual. The men in the club were smoking, telling off-color jokes and playing a bit of poker. It was just like any other night in the club, or so it seemed.

Inspector Valentine had set his trap carefully and there was nothing left to chance. All had been prepared in strictest accordance with the law. The police had learned of the gambling from the complaints of wives of men who had lost their pay in the club and could not put food on the table for their kids. Detective Moe Glatterman swore that he had visited the club several times during February and had placed bets under the alias of Gerhardt. Detective Glatterman even testified that on one occasion McGuinness himself had entered the club and ordered it cleared because of "the cops."

Valentine approached Chief Magistrate William McAdoo for a warrant to raid the club. The police submitted affidavits to the judge that gamblers had full sway in McGuinness' club. The police played tapes of wiretaps in which Pete and known bookies were heard accepting bets. Judge McAdoo concluded that there was sufficient evidence of organized gambling and issued the warrant. The last piece was then in place and finally the trap could be sprung.

Suddenly, the people in the club heard the heavy thud of feet on double time running up the stairs to the club. The police kicked open the door and yelled, "Police! Nobody move." The cops immediately grabbed the Kirwan brothers, but they were more interested in the big fish on the second floor of the club. The cops bolted upstairs to arrest Alderman McGuinness, and most importantly, seize the contents of the safe in his private office. One of the cops cried out, "Make sure no one has a chance to close the safe." There was a din of shouting. Some of the cops began turning over tables and grabbing bookie sheets.

When the alderman saw the police, some reported he cried out, "Cheese it boys; it's the cops." McGuinness was found hiding behind a pillar, arrested and charged with bookmaking. The police continued to ransack the place and quickly ripped the phones out of the wall on the lower floor. Some of the men in the club cried out, "Pete we wasn't gambling and they can't arrest us," but McGuinness, told them not to resist, promising he would get to the bottom of the whole affair. The police were daunted by the task of booking more than a hundred prisoners. Quickly though, they began to march them down the stairs and out of the building.

The scene outside the club was total bedlam and there was danger of a riot. Men were shouting threats at the police. The police, though, had been well prepared for the arrests. They had stopped traffic on Manhattan Avenue for a block on either side of Meserole Avenue where the club was located. Only after the raid had begun did they call the local precincts, asking for reinforcements to form a perimeter around the club. Dozens of people from the area, including many of the wives and girlfriends of the club members, came running to the club and formed a menacing and verbally abusive crowd beyond the perimeter, but the precinct was only two doors away. When the arrested men were marched out a torrent of taunts greeted the officers. Booking in the station was a scene of near pandemonium.

Word spread like wildfire around Greenpoint. Quickly, it was learned that two other political clubs, the Wigwam Club down the street on Manhattan Avenue and Registrar McQuade's club right opposite McGuinness' club on Manhattan and Meserole, were also raided for gambling, though McQuade was not in his club during the raid.

Many people who never read *The New York Times* eagerly awaited its morning edition to find out exactly what had happened. McGuinness had always loved being in the papers, but that morning's coverage angered him. His arrest was front-page news and the *Times* headline read:

Alderman Seized in Gambling Raids

And the byline read:

Fighting McGuinness Arrested along with 158 Others in Democratic Clubs

The article explained that the arrests were the result of Chief of Police McLaughlin's use of wiretaps. The report said that Alderman McGuinness, known as "The Fighting Greenpoint Alderman," was arrested on a charge of bookmaking. It explained that eight men, in addition to McGuinness, were arrested on the bookmaking charge and that about a hundred and fifty others were arrested for disorderly conduct. The article stated that all were released on bail at the police station and that they would all be arraigned this morning at the Bridge Street Courthouse. The article informed New Yorkers that inspector Thomas McDonald had been in charge of the raids and that fifteen detectives had taken part in them.

The *Times* informed readers that warrants for the arrest of McGuinness and the other bookmakers had been signed by Chief City Magistrate William McAdoo. Readers learned that the greatest secrecy about the warrants had been maintained and that no word of them had leaked out. The *Times* reported that Inspector McDonald, fearing the politician's connections with the police in his own district would serve as a grapevine to tip them off, took great care not to let the local precincts know anything about the raids. The raiding detectives borrowed patrol wagons and uniformed officers from other precincts without revealing their plans for using them.

The *Times* article related that when the detectives were sure that the men they wanted were in the club, they descended on them suddenly, taking them by surprise. According to the *Times* account, Alderman McGuinness expressed himself indignantly to the policemen, but refused to make a statement to the press. He was bailed out by his brother George. The *Times* noted that Registrar McQuade, the bitter political enemy of McGuinness, offered to put up the bond for the alderman's release, even though the two have led rival factions in the Greenpoint Democratic Party.

The article did not tell readers that McGuinness was furious both with the police commissioner and with Mayor Walker, whom he had fervently supported. After being released, McGuinness immediately rushed off to confront the Mayor, who was taking part in a black tie affair, called the Inner Circle, at the Hotel Astor in Manhattan. Pete strode across the ballroom floor with large, menacing steps that showed his fury. He confronted the Mayor with a torrent of abuse about McLaughlin. The Mayor tried to calm the large, menacing alderman's ire, but to little avail. One of the police officials singing at the Inner Circle evening sought to provoke McGuinness even further. He had heard of the raid and dedicated a little ditty to McGuinness that he had just composed. He sang, "Although gambling dens for years I've been suppressing and at stopping games of chance I am no dub. The commissioner this time had me guessing when he ordered me to pull a McGuinness club." The singing cop laughed maliciously and Pete might have socked him in the face had he not been restrained.

Pete called the arrest, "a dirty low-down frame up," proclaiming loudly that he had never gambled in his life, let alone done any bookmaking, and he was livid because the raid was in his eyes strictly political. He knew that the raid would be headline news for all his constituents and that his political future was now in grave doubt.

The next day he was arraigned by a lifelong friend and political ally, Judge James Short, at the Bridge Plaza Court. When the charges were read to him, Pete laughed, calling them ludicrous. Judge Short dismissed the charges for lack of evidence. The scene in the courtroom was one of the most chaotic the judge had ever seen in all his years on the bench. All of the hundred and fifty-nine men arrested in the raid were in the court, along with many of their friends, family and, of course, lawyers. There was real anger in the room that threatened to explode at any moment. There was nearly a brawl when one of the released prisoners brushed up against one of the detectives and hissed at him, "You rat." The detective had to be restrained, as did the arrested man.

McGuinness asked to speak later in the day on the floor of City Hall at a meeting of the aldermen. He again repeated his claim that he was innocent and that the arrests were politically motivated. He called for the Board of Aldermen to do a thorough investigation of the raid of his club.

McGuinness, however, had not seen the worst of the headlines. On March 17 there was very little luck of the Irish for McGuinness. The *Times* ran a front-page article with a headline that announced:

McGuinness Safe Yields $114, 000 in Bets

This was especially damaging in a blue-collar area like Greenpoint where people may have brought home twenty-five to thirty dollars a week. The headline also said that there was an annual take of $600,000 a year and a yearly profit to the bookmakers of $60,000. The article revealed that the betting records were found in the safe, which was in an office that only McGuinness and the gamblers had access to. McLaughlin in a statement to the press then asked the question that was surely on everyone's mind: "Who gets this money? Do the professional gamblers retain all of it? If so, it will be well to know what an extraordinary privilege they enjoy at the club."

McGuinness' rise to political power was based on the belief that he was "as clean as a whistle." Obviously, the headlines were ammunition for McGuinness' opponents, but even his supporters also began to doubt his claims of honesty. Many people accused Pete of being in cahoots with the gamblers and believed that he was getting a take of the massive profits. Obviously, Pete had to clear his name, but it would take Pete years to prove his honesty and other allegations would increase the perception that Pete was implicated in the rackets. McGuinness' enemies relished the idea that his reign as "King of Greenpoint" would soon end, and they gleefully looked forward to his fall.

Chapter Five: The Aftermath March 14, 1927

Greenpoint talked about nothing else except the raid. All week long all the papers, even *The New York Times,* ran stories about it. McGuinness supporters argued heatedly in public places with his detractors. A seventy-year-old man was arrested when he punched his lifelong friend in the nose for calling McGuinness a crook. Several similar battles doubtless occurred, but went unreported. Many Greenpointers rallied to his defense and felt that there was nothing wrong with gambling and that their beloved McGuinness was being set up.

The scandalous arrest of Alderman McGuinness was front-page news in *The Brooklyn Daily Eagle* the following day. The headline declared:

McLaughlin Told McGuinness to End Gambling

Underneath the headline it stated that the alderman

had been warned to end bookmaking in his club. The *Eagle* printed in bold type a heading that gamblers had full sway and they used McGuinness' clubs as a means of evading arrest. McLaughlin also told the *Eagle* that the police had made repeated requests to stop the gambling, which were ignored, and that the scope of gambling was actually increasing at the time of the raid, which was testified to by the fact that there were a hundred and fifty men in the club at the time of the raid. He continued saying that McGuinness was well aware of the fact that professional gamblers were using his club to break the law, but he never acted to stop it. He stated that every attempt was made to have the gambling discontinued, but without success. To rub salt in McGuinness' wounds, the commissioner added that Brooklyn Democratic Leader John McCooey co-operated fully with the police and that he was eager to stamp out illegal gambling in political clubs. Finally, McLaughlin shot back at McGuinness with a statement that was reported by all the papers, saying, "The threatened investigation to be instigated by Alderman McGuinness will be most welcomed as it would give us an opportunity to submit facts that would not ordinarily be brought out in a court proceeding."

McGuinness played the role of victim, saying, "I have never gambled in my life. I have never bet so much as a nickel, nor accepted the bet of a nickel." He claimed that you could find bookmaking anywhere, even in Police Headquarters. He also stated that he planned to sue for false arrest, saying that he was singled-out simply because he was a high profile target, and also stating, "If it had been anybody else's club they wouldn't have mentioned it in the papers, but its Pete McGuinness's club and they'll have it all over the front page. You do a lot of good in the world and they do not give you a break, but if you get off the path, then your name is all over the papers, especially if your name is Peter McGuinness." He told the *Eagle* that he was amazed at the action of the police in raiding his clubhouse. The alderman claimed that he would pay anyone a hundred dollars who could prove that he had ever taken any kind of a bet. McGuinness produced a slew of invitations from the racetrack's Jockey Club for free visits, but Pete said that he had turned them all down because he did not gamble.

Pete vowed that he would bring the commissioner to his knees for the raid and he pressured his friend and ally, Mayor Jimmy Walker, to fire the upstart police commissioner.

The story remained in each day's headline for a week and each day's headline damaged further Pete's credibility. A female reporter asked McGuinness if he had shared in the large take the police found in his safe. McGuinness looked at her with irritation and said, "My dear young lady if I ever made $60,000 in the gambling game I would be riding around in a ritzy car and looking like a swell dude."

Pete had risen to power as an anti-corruption reformer, vowing to stamp out graft and bring honest government to Greenpoint. He had always prided himself on his honesty. Now circumstantial evidence seemed to contradict that narrative. If McGuinness could not answer the damaging allegations surrounding the raid on his club and his arrest for gambling, then his political reputation would be sullied and his career would be over.

On the eighteenth the *Eagle* returned to the club for an exclusive report. The club was in full damage control mode. The members of the club rallied behind Pete, defending him vigorously. One of the club members averred that there was not a more honest man anywhere in the world than Pete McGuinness. Another member announced that he believed that Pete had never gambled on the horses in his whole long life.

The *Eagle* said that the club meeting on March 18 could have passed for a Sunday school gathering. All the people interviewed in the club said that not only did the people of the neighborhood believe that the raid was a frame-up by McLaughlin, but also that Pete would actually gain from the publicity that the raid created. The *Eagle* reporter noted that unlike the night of the raid when there were only men in the club, now the club was not only represented by women, but that all the prettiest girls in Greenpoint seemed to be in the club.

One of the members told a reporter that he could still see just how popular McGuinness still was in Greenpoint by coming back next week for the annual McGuinness charity ball. He said that he was sure that five thousand people would show up for the affair and that he would give the reporter even money and then, suddenly remembering that the club had been raided for gambling, he grew tongue-tied, blushed and broke off his offer in mid-sentence.

McGuinness did get some support from some journalists. The *New York Business Press* bucked the trend of attacking the alderman and wrote of his "being one of the real leaders of the city in its civic life and that he had evidently been made the goat of interests averse to him." Ex-Alderman Harvey called the arrest a "frame-up" in the same article.

No one was happier about the raid than McGuinness' archenemy, Registrar James McQuade. Even though his own club had been raided and evidence of bookmaking had been seized, McQuade reacted with glee. The arrest seemed to confirm what the registrar had been saying all along, namely that McGuinness was not fit to be either alderman or district leader. He rubbed his hands in delight at the thought of all the political hay he could make out of McGuinness' arrest. Perhaps the people would now see through McGuinness and they would re-elect him to the post he had always wanted back: district leader.

Chapter Six: McGuinness as Early Greenpoint Historian

Dear Reader, with your permission, we are going to set aside for a few chapters the story of Pete's 1931 arrest and step back in time to place McGuinness' tale in the wider context of Greenpoint history. However, if you are enjoying McGuinness' character and fear that he will depart the narrative, rest easy. McGuinness will guide us through Greenpoint history in his own entertaining way and then we will resume the interrupted story of his arrest. Greenpoint had a history every bit as unique as McGuinness himself and Pete's one-of-a-kind personality could only have been created there.

During the Great Depression of the 1930's life was hard and the newspapers wanted to cheer people up. No one was funnier than Peter McGuinness, and the papers consulted him about a variety of subjects because he had humorous opinions on all of them. In 1936, as Brooklyn anticipated its three hundredth anniversary of European settlement, there was an intense argument amongst historians regarding the areas of Flatlands and Flatbush could make the claim to be Brooklyn's first settlement. Scholars visited archives and checked ancient dusty Dutch records to settle the dispute.

If the scholars were unsure about early Brooklyn history, then McGuinness was not. Unlike the wavering academics, McGuinness had settled the dispute conclusively and was certain that Greenpoint was Brooklyn's first European settlement. *The Daily Eagle* noted, "Sheriff Peter J. McGuinness entered the controversy by claiming that the first white settler in Brooklyn established a home in Greenpoint, the Garden Spot of the World." The *Eagle* article stated, "Should Sheriff McGuinness confirm that statement today it is declared possible that all existing borough histories may be scrapped for none of them point to Greenpoint as the landing place of the first white settler."

According to historians, because of its geographic isolation, Greenpoint lagged behind other areas of Brooklyn, remaining rural and isolated long after other areas had become settled towns. If McGuinness ever read any of these accounts of Greenpoint's delayed development, then he dismissed them completely. He once opined on Greenpoint history, "Greenpoint was a city when Brooklyn was just a lot of trees and shrubs. Greenpoint made

Brooklyn and you know what New York would be without Brooklyn, just a puddle; that's all."

By the 1940s, McGuinness was famous not only in Greenpoint, but all over Brooklyn, for his hyperbolic statements about Greenpoint. The president of the Flatbush Chamber of Commerce, Ben King, challenged McGuinness to a historical debate, which was reported in two humorous articles in *The Brooklyn Daily Eagle*, as to which area was older: Greenpoint or Flatbush. McGuinness defended Greenpoint and added, "When I get through showing them how long Greenpoint has been settled, they'll be sorry they ever started the discussion." He added, "Irishmen from Greenpoint had to come to Flatbush years ago and beat up the Indians so that white people could settle there and now this Irishman will come to Flatbush and beat Ben King in the debate so that this question can now be settled."

King disputed Greenpoint's claim of 1636 settlement on the north side of Bushwick Creek by Dirck Volckertszen, saying that the first house was only built in Greenpoint in 1646 and that house was only one hundred feet by two hundred feet,

"Hardly big enough for a Flatbush man to expand his chest." McGuinness countered saying, "The Greenpoint inhabitants were always patriotic and paved the way for the settlement of Brooklyn." King then leveled the false claim that during the revolution there were only eight families in Greenpoint (actually there were five) and that no Greenpoint soldier had gone to the Battle of Brooklyn to fight the British. McGuinness, boarding a train to Albany, had time only for one final salvo, noting that Flatbush was so backwards that "It wasn't let into the county until a hundred years ago."

A man from Flatlands joined the historical fray when Louis Elder wrote a letter to the *Daily Eagle* not only claiming that Brooklyn was named by the freeholders of Flatlands, but also that Greenpoint and Flatbush were "minor communities" in Brooklyn! Luckily for Elder, he was not within McGuinness' long reach, because McGuinness could become violent in defense of Greenpoint. He once said, "Brooklyn is the greatest community that was ever made up in the world. If anybody ever insults it, smack 'em in the eye."

A generation before the debate, Greenpoint had become conscious of its long history. In 1915, when McGuinness was twenty-six years old, the Greenpoint Savings Bank published the first Greenpoint history: *Historic Greenpoint*. The author, William Felter, a Native Greenpointer and Brooklyn Girls High School Principal, most likely knew McGuinness because they were active in the same civic clubs. McGuinness must have read Felter's book. Perhaps Felter's book encouraged McGuinness' belief in Greenpoint's historical importance. Pete once humorously claimed that no place in America had more history than Greenpoint.

Felter's history, though groundbreaking, made terrible omissions, leaving out ecological destruction, labor strikes and the numerous fires that destroyed so much property and took many lives. Felter's book is also replete with fulsome praise of local slave owners and industrialists and its tone verges on jingoism. For example, he celebrates the first European Greenpointer, Dirck the Norseman, while dismissing his destruction of the Native Americans and his introduction of African slavery into the area. It's a celebration of the march of progress in Greenpoint with no mention of industrial development's massive damage. In fairness to the author, the bank would not have paid him money to write a balanced account of the development of Greenpoint.

In 1924, an incident occurred that aroused local interest in early colonial Greenpoint history. Workers digging a gas main on Morgan Avenue discovered remnants of a seventeenth century boat and dock. In an article about the discovery in *The Brooklyn Daily Eagle*—a reporter interviewed Felter, who stated that these were archeological remains belonged to the first Greenpoint settler, Dirck the Norseman. The discovery renewed interest in Greenpoint's settlement. Pete must have been amused because, ironically enough, like McGuinness, Volckertszen worked with lumber. He was both a house and ship's carpenter who came to Greenpoint to cut timber intermittently before settling there permanently.

There was another similarity that people during Prohibition would have found ironic. Volckertszen was a smuggler, and part of the reason he settled in Greenpoint was that its isolated location helped his smuggling operations avoid the prying eyes of Dutch customs agents. In the 1920s, during prohibition, it was not Dutch customs agents Greenpointers were avoiding, but federal agents, looking for alcohol. No place in America was a bigger center for bootlegging than Greenpoint, and Canadian booze was regularly smuggled into Greenpoint, not very far from the very spot on Franklin and Calyer Street where Dirck built the first settlement.

Eventually, Dirck and the first Scandinavian settlers sold their holdings to one of the five Huguenot families who farmed the land, intermarried with each other and lived in splendid isolation for about one hundred and fifty years. These Huguenot families gave their names to some of the local streets—Calyer, Meserole and Provost—and in Pete's day the remnants of Greenpoint's agricultural past were still present—Adrian Meserole, a descendent of one of these families and one of the founders of the Green Point Savings Bank that published Felter's book, lived until 1913 in his family's colonial-era seventeen-room mansion on Lorimer Street. It's quite likely that Pete knew Meserole and learned a lot of Greenpoint history from him.

Meserole must have told him about the famous family orchard that he cut down and sold off in lots, making him a millionaire. The Orchard's eastern boundary was Leonard Street, right where Pete would later reside for many years. Adrian cut Meserole Avenue, the future site of McGuinness' clubhouse, through the heart of this orchard.

The Orchard, famed for its beauty, was referred to as a "garden spot." Years later, when the beauty of the orchard was little more than a memory, Pete referred to Greenpoint as "The Garden Spot of the Universe," and the name stuck, despite the fact that Meserole had cut down his orchard long ago. Meserole's land sales transformed this romantic beauty spot into a drab, heavily industrialized and polluted area.

Felter, McGuinness and most Greenpoint natives shared a strong historical sense. They knew that their area had a unique past and they were proud of it. However, people were not proudest of the early past. They were proudest about a curious, locally built ship that changed American history and put Greenpoint on the map.

Chapter Seven: McGuinness Rewrites History

McGuinness was more than an influential political figure. He was also a revisionist historian who revised not only Brooklyn colonial history, but also Greenpoint's most important event—the 1862 Construction of the first ironclad battleship that ever fought in battle—John Ericsson's revolutionary battleship, the Monitor. McGuinness' version of the battle might not have been entirely accurate, but it was, like most of his versions, highly amusing.

Greenpoint had long celebrated the famous ship and the historic Battle of Hampton Roads in which the Monitor saved the Union Navy by fighting the confederate ironclad ship, the Virginia, to a standstill, thus preventing the Confederacy from breaking the Union blockade, winning the war and continuing slavery. Let's allow Pete to narrate history. It was March 9, 1937, the seventy-fifth anniversary of the battle, and McGuinness was speaking to a local crowd that amazingly included senior citizens who had seen the construction of the futuristic ship as children. McGuinness said:

> We celebrate this day the memory of a great ship that was built right here in our midst right down at the Continental Iron Works at West and Calyer Streets. (Actually the Continental Iron works was at Quay Street, not Calyer, but no one in the crowd dared interrupt McGuinness.) "It was back in 1861 and we in the North were in a peculiar position. The South had a boat made of iron with a bow in the front that could plow up our boats, put the water in and sink them.

McGuinness next spoke about the designer of the futuristic Monitor, Swedish born naval engineer John Ericsson, whom everyone in the audience knew, but who deserves an introduction here. In 1862, Ericsson was living in a boarding house on Calyer Street while overseeing the construction of his ship at the Continental Iron Works, one of the few places anywhere in 1862 capable of building an iron ship. The United States Navy had wrongly blackballed Ericsson sixteen years previously. He had designed a futuristic ship called the Princeton for an unscrupulous American entrepreneur named John Stockton. The Princeton was like no other ship afloat. Steam and propeller powered it, not wind. Ericsson designed most of the ship, yet Stockton robbed Ericsson of the credit for it, claiming the design was his own. Stockton, though, in fact, designed the one flawed part of the ship, a huge naval gun that exploded on the ship's maiden voyage, scandalously killing many Washington dignitaries. Although, Stockton, not Ericsson, was to blame for the blast, Stockton influenced the Navy's investigation of the disaster, and amazingly Ericsson took the blame Stockton rightly deserved. Ericsson was erroneously told he would never build another navy ship.

McGuinness continued the Monitor story: "John Ericsson tried to give the Navy the idea, but the men in command turned it down." He explained how Lincoln himself had overridden his own admirals. McGuinnes said, "Abraham Lincoln said, 'the gold braids have turned their back on something that might help us.' So Abraham Lincoln sent for him and ordered the boat built and Ericsson built it right here in Greenpoint."

Though the victory of the Monitor was historically significant, no historian ever explained the importance of the battle in the fulsome terms McGuinness did, stating, "The ship saved the union. They called it a cheese box on a raft, but they might have called it a hunk of cheese. It wouldn't have made a whiff of difference. The boat won the war almost single handed." He continued, "She wasn't as big as some out protecting our coast today, but she done her work just as good and we in Greenpoint should be proud." McGuinness had already had the anniversary of the battle made a New York State holiday called "Monitor Day," but he wanted more. He said in reference to the March ninth holiday, "It should be a national holiday. Our great president should take over the Continental Iron Works site and make a historic park there, for it was at that spot that our government found our iron ships were good in conflict with other nations and she showed while she was small in size she done a tremendous lot of work in saving our nation and our president." McGuinness stated, "Greenpoint has not only given to the nation, but she has given good."

McGuinness showed that he was no nitpicker for dates when it came to his proposed holiday. He was willing to change the date of the engagement to summer. He said, "I remember that we had the celebration two years ago in front of the iron works and we were all out there with ear muffs on. And this morning it rained and this afternoon it snowed and tonight's cold so we had to have the celebration indoors. Why the hell didn't this battle take place in July and August so we could all be there and have a good time?"

McGuinness fought for funds to build a statue that was approved and dedicated three years later in 1938. McGuinnness had asked for fifteen thousand dollars, but Greenpoint only received $5,000. McGuinness was irate at the funding cut and outraged that larger sums went to build a statue of General Grant. He stated, "Let me tell you that General Grant wouldn't have amounted to a hill of beans if it had not been for the little Monitor and the Garden Spot of the Universe." McGuinness summed up his remarks saying, "If it hadn't been for Greenpoint there wouldn't be a United States of America today and that's why I am fighting to get this here monument to commemorate the construction of the Monitor."

In 1938, thanks to McGuinness' efforts, a bronze statute dedicated to Ericsson and his revolutionary battleship was dedicated in Winthrop Park. Italian Antonio De Fillipo cast a figure pulling a hawser with the hull of the ship beneath him. An inscription beneath the statue read:

> ERECTED BY THE PEOPLE OF THE / STATE OF NEW YORK / TO COMMEMORATE THE BATTLE OF THE / MONITOR AND MERRIMAC / MARCH

9TH, 1862 / AND IN MEMORY / OF THE MEN OF THE MONITOR / AND ITS DESIGNER — JOHN ERICSSON

McGuinness knew Greenpoint history and he was aware that the area had been a center for shipyards long before Ericsson built the Monitor. In his 1940 debate with Ben King of the Flatbush Chamber of Commerce, when the Flatbush merchant tried to belittle Greenpoint's historical role, McGuinness correctly pointed out to him that there was no more important neighborhood for shipbuilding than Greenpoint and the Flatbush man had to agree, although Bell sarcastically noted that lifeboats were the most widely manufactured ships the area built.

In the 1830s, a Manhattan shipbuilder named Neziah Bliss realized that a booming Manhattan would displace the shipyards that lined the East River shoreline. Looking across the river and realizing that Greenpoint farmland would be perfect for a waterfront shipbuilding community, Bliss purchased thirty acres of riverfront property and even married the homely daughter of Revolutionary War hero John Meserole to acquire even more land. Bliss had the land surveyed and had streets laid out. Donating some of his land holdings so that a ferry could be established, he also built the first bridge over Bushwick Creek, establishing a direct link with Williamsburg and ending the area's historic isolation from the rest of Brooklyn.

By the late 1840s, a small shipbuilding community was emerging and Greenpoint saw the construction of its first ship in 1850. Quickly shipyards lined the East River waterfront and the shoreline around West Street was extended with landfill. Many of the first area residents were shipwrights and other people whose professions were related to shipbuilding. Bliss died in 1876, twelve years before McGuinness was born, but McGuinness and many of his neighbors worked on the waterfront Bliss envisioned.

The Civil War witnessed the heyday of local shipbuilding, but shipbuilding declined rapidly after the war. However, even after ship construction faded, the waterfront played a vital role in the life of the community. A local Irish family, the McAllisters, founded a tugboat and lighter firm that would attract many Irish people from Cushendall, County Antrim, to Greenpoint, and McGuinness grew up with the children of these Irish immigrants. Local shipyards required wood and brass, which would also affect McGuinness. Brass was an integral element in shipbuilding, and McGuinness' father relocated from New Jersey to work in a local brass factory where he became foreman and spent forty years of his life. Even after shipbuilding's decline, the lumberyards, which supplied shipbuilders timber, remained, and Pete's first adult job was in Orr's Lumber Yard. Greenpoint became the center for lumber in New York, and woodworking today still remains an important local industry.

As a result of Bliss' vision, Greenpoint developed along its working waterfront. Many of the people who settled there worked in industries related to shipbuilding, and the sailors, tugboat pilots and longshoremen who worked its waterfront were tough, unique, colorful characters like Pete. Although the waterfront would remain important, the advent of other industries would have a far more profound influence on the character of the area.

Chapter Eight: The Birth of Industrial Greenpoint and Its Working Class

McGuinness grew up in one of the largest industrial areas in the world and was intensely proud of being a working-class Greenpointer. He was also proud of the role Greenpoint's industries played in the development of America. Greenpoint was called "the American Birmingham" because its factories produced so many different products. Newtown Creek became one of the busiest waterways in the country and it once had more industrial output than the entire Mississippi River, though it was far shorter. McGuinnes believed that Greenpoint's industry had played a vital role in America's greatness saying, "When history is wrote and rewrote Greenpoint is going to have its share of the credit."

The Greenpointers like Peter who worked in these local industries were blue-collar workers, far different than their genteel, upper-class neighbors in other parts of the borough. They were a no-nonsense group who worked hard and were proud of it. McGuinness' language was Brooklynese, the speech of the workers, and he and his neighbors spoke differently than more educated Brooklynites. In fact, the locals spoke their own proletarian dialect, Greenpoint Brooklynese, and McGuinness was very proud of speaking it. It is surprising that McGuinness, with only a grammar- school education, was an expert on Brooklyn history, but it is even more amazing that Peter was a linguistic theoretician who was an expert on the Garden Spot's mores, folkways and habits of speech.

He shared his accumulated linguistic research and findings with the local press. *The Brooklyn Daily Eagle* in a March 15, 1935 article wanted McGuinness to explain, "the strange magic that distinguishes the language in Greenpoint from more prosaic communities." McGuinness was an ardent linguistic patriot and felt that Americans need not worry about following British English, stating, "Now what do you think them fellers in 1776 signed the declaration of Independence for if they wanted to stay with England. Ain't we got a good enough language? I mean American, without talking the King's English."

McGuinness, at the time of his interview, was an official in Borough Hall on Court Street surrounded by articulate people who used high-sounding erudite phrases, and the reporter asked him if listening to such educated men had not wrought the slightest improvement in his own speech. The question offended him, and he maintained that he still pronounced words in the strictest Greenpointian tradition. Any change, he averred, would be almost treasonous. He said to the bearded interviewer, “You can bet every one of those hairs on yer chin I ain’t goin’ to dude up my talk.” He continued, “When I talk people won’t have to run home and pick up a Webster’s dictionary to know what I am saying.” He added, “I always say that it aint the wrapper around the package; its what’s inside that counts. I know some fellers as talks all day with a lot of flowers coming out of their mouths and they ain’t saying nothing at all.”

The reporter pressed McGuinness to analyze the unique phonology of Grenepoint speech, and he said, “Well out in Greenpoint we don’t sound our r’s so sharp like. We bring ‘em out nice and flat.” Word, became woid; the, I, in the word, voice, would come out like an r so it would sound like verse. McGuinness summed up by saying he felt that he and his fellow Greenpointers spoke the most authentic American language. He said, “It’s our duty to speak the American language.”

Greenpoint, though, had not always been industrial.

It had once been such a natural beauty spot that Manhattanites traveled over by ferry to picnic on top of its pretty hills. They enjoyed the numerous wildflowers that grew on Pottery Hill, not far from where McGuinness was born, but by the time of his birth, Greenpoint had become heavily industrialized and polluted. People lived tooth and jowl with a huge array of highly toxic, dangerous factories. The neighborhood became the home to "the Five Black Arts," which included oil refineries, iron foundries, printing, glass factories and porcelain production. Other industries included the production of pencils, rope, boxes, electrical outlets and a list too long to recite.

Before industrialization, Newtown Creek was a clean body of water whose bottom was covered with clams and oysters. The creek teemed with schools of fish that included sea bass, shad and porgies. Until the 1870s, local boys grew up swimming in the limpid waters of Newtown Creek and diving off the docks into the East River. Pete, though, was of a later generation and he never knew the creek to be anything other than a foul, heavily polluted body of often-putrid water.

Charles Pratt opened his Astral Oil Works locally in 1867, the first modern oil refinery in America, which both produced huge amounts of oil and made Pratt Brooklyn's richest man. However, it also destroyed the local environment. Pratt would secretly form a cartel with John D. Rockefeller and sit on the board of Standard Oil. Dozens of other refineries opened locally, all equally as destructive. By 1880, Rockefeller controlled over one hundred stills along Newtown Creek, which employed two thousand workers, producing three million gallons of crude oil each week, but when petroleum was moved from distillery to wharf to schooner, it often spilled and companies also discarded unwanted byproducts simply by dumping them into the creek. Over fifty other businesses along Newtown Creek processed kerosene, coal, paraffin wax, chemicals, fertilizers and lumber, producing the equivalent of 300,000 gallons of waste material each week during the 1880s, much of which made its way into local waterways. Quickly, millions of gallons of oil from storage tanks leaked into the creek and soon, when kids went swimming they emerged from the creek covered in thick black goo.

Perhaps Pratt suffered from a bad conscience because destruction of Greenpoint's ecology had made him a multimillionaire. He dedicated his life to philanthropy, and he rewarded his poorly housed workers by building the landmark Astral Building in 1883, five years before McGuinness' birth. The Astral was a revolutionary building—the first model apartment house a company built only for its workers. The building cost a fortune and was meant to be a showcase. The same architectural firm that built Theodore Roosevelt's home at Sagamore Hill and Barnard College designed the gorgeous Queen Anne-style façade of the building. It had large well-lit ventilated apartments and even had toilets in the basement, an unheard-of luxury. Pratt even funded a settlement house that taught classes on every subject from English language to home economics. He even condescendingly constructed a model home nearby, so that Greenpointers could see how supposedly "decent" people lived.

McGuinness actually boarded in the Astral for a short time as a young man when his family temporarily moved out of Greenpoint, and the building was the scene of a funny teenage story McGuinness told all his life. There was another handsome young man named John McGuinness (no relation) who was dating a local girl, and he decided to take her to the top of the Astral building for a rendezvous. The girl's mother received a frightening report, "McGuinness is with your daughter."

The enraged mother, fearing for her daughter's reputation, hurried to the Astral with the fury of a banshee, determined to find her daughter and oblivious to the fact that Peter was blameless. When the irate mother arrived at the corner of Java and Franklin she found Pete

McGuinness, not John, standing innocently, dressed in his best hat and suit. McGuinness' ignorance about her daughter's whereabouts so infuriated the mother that she attacked him physically. Peter, too much of a gentleman to hit a lady, tried to fend off the woman's numerous punches, kicks and other blows. At the end of the attack Pete's new white hat, which had been stomped on, lay crushed on the floor. His hair was a mess and many of the buttons on his shirt and jacket had been ripped off. John McGuinness and his girlfriend watched the entire attack unfold from the roof of the Astral with great amusement, but never descended to help the embattled Peter.

Newtown Creek became so polluted that the once-pristine body of water had become unrecognizable. It was home to putrid fertilizer plants, chemical works, and factories that processed animal bones. The sludge oil that was a by-product of fertilizer stank to high heaven, and frequently the winds that blew from the east carried the stench across to affluent Murray Hill in Manhattan. McGuinness did all he could to fight the stench in Greenpoint, but Pete always had a sense of humor. Someone once asked him about the pollution of the area and its effects on people's health. He replied, "Greenpoint is the healthiest place on earth. The fumes from the East River kill all the germs and the people in our place are hardened to the fumes."

By the 1880's, *The New York Times* began to report with increasing regularity on the stenches wafting over the East River. "On warm sunny days, a quivering envelope of nauseous fog hangs above the place like a pall of death," the paper reported in 1887. It noted how the sludge acid mixed with decaying fish, flesh and all sorts of offal and described how refuse from the plants was dumped into Newtown Creek whence it readily found its way into the East River, covering this water thickly with a greasy poisonous substance.

During the 1890s, local activists, calling themselves the Fifteenth Ward Smelling Committee, paddled up the creek, seeking the polluters responsible for the foul stenches wafting from the once-pristine waterway. They had plenty to choose from: glue-makers and fertilizer processors produced plenty of noxious by-products, but the oil refineries were the worst offenders. As they sailed up the creek the committee members passed reeking manure scows. Floating by the dog pound and sausage factories, they were revolted to see heaps of flesh baking in the open sun. Sludge acid, a tarlike substance produced by refineries, emitted an odor that could "nauseate a horse." The smell grew worse and worse, until they reached the refineries themselves, where "The odors began asserting themselves with all the vigor of fully developed stenches."

When the local Enoch Coe Fertilizer Company was prosecuted for its production of noxious odors, no one in the courtroom was brave enough to remove the stopper from a bottle of its sludge acid. The *Times* also noted that the area was the worst-smelling district in the world, and reported on the Long Island Railroad's journey to Hunter's Point, "The waters of Newtown Creek run through a region that gives out more disgusting smells per square inch than any other portion of the world can furnish in a square mile." The article also stated, "There is not a man, woman or child who travels the Long Island Railroad who will not testify to the horrible nature of the smells, which assail the passengers during their journey along Newtown Creek."

A special Committee of the New York State Health Department did a fact-finding mission along the creek and reported that the creek was so full of oil and refuse that the water almost had the consistency of tar. When visiting one of the plants that mixed water with sludge acid, the odor was so strong that Assemblyman Brooks, who was along with the delegation, commented that the power of the smell was as if, "a knife had pierced him after taking one whiff." Working-class Greenpointers like

McGuinness did not dwell on the pollution, or its effects on their health. They made light of it. Despite the pollution, Pete always referred to his area humorously as, "the Garden Spot".

Once a journalist asked him if he would invite Congressman Zioncheck to Greenpoint. He replied:

> Never, a thousand times never! If he gets one glance at Greenpoint, the Garden Spot of the Universe, inhales our invigorating fresh air, views our unsurpassable landscape, he'll make posthaste to Washington to have laws enacted to transplant Greenpoint right beside the Capitol. What has Washington got that we haven't got? Cherry blossoms? Phooey! That display they make a fuss about down there looks like an amateur contest for horticulturists besides the real blooming stuff you see in Greenpoint.

Chapter Nine: Danger Town

McGuinness' legendary toughness sprang in part from growing up in the most dangerous part of Greenpoint, an area that ran from Ash Street to Huron Street around Oakland Street, so scary it was called "Danger Town." The area frightened others, but McGuinness, a huge boxer, did not see it that way. He said, "Greenpoint was never known as a tough place. Never in the world. Greenpoint never has been tough and never will be, but not sissy either." However, he was not really telling the truth. By the 1880s, Greenpoint had changed from a community of prosperous, well-paid shipwrights into a place with pockets of overcrowded tenements and dangerous social conditions. Danger Town became synonymous with alcoholism, gang violence and juvenile delinquency.

The area's depravity scandalized *The Brooklyn Daily Eagle,* which did reports on the shocking conditions there. The paper described the area as a hotbed of crime and a den of thieves. In an 1886 expose, it claimed that gangs and "jail birds" infested the area, stating, "Were it not for the protection of the cops of the Seventh Precinct it would be dangerous to walk there, even during daytime." The gangs had colorful names, calling themselves "the Policemen killers," "the Danger Town Slobs," "the Sons of Rest" and 'the Jolly Four." The report described the area as a "plague," claiming that nine-tenths of the crime in Greenpoint was the work of Danger Town toughs, with every kind of crime committed there. The *Eagle* reported that many of the gang members were homeless young men who slept nights in horse barns on Oakland Street.

The *Eagle* also said that Danger Town was a place full of bars with two or three on every block and that people there did no work other than robbing and drinking growlers of beer. The *Eagle* report also claimed that area's thieves sole thought was how to make a "haul" of a well-filled purse, to spend on more growlers. Several pedestrians on the streets near the dumps were "stood up" for the requisite amount of money, and after the "growler" had been worked several times the boys were, "ready for anything from robbing a bobtail car driver to assaulting the police."

Another *Brooklyn Daily Eagle* article reported the Danger Town dump, which not long ago had been the pretty Back Meadow, had quickly grown into ten or twelve acres full of ash and filthy refuse. Goats, cows and pigs roamed the dump, while Italian rag pickers and small boys trooped over it, finding, "wonderful treasures." The Italians came from New York and the police of the Seventh Precinct had to keep an eye on them to prevent them from being stoned to death by the loitering gangs on the borders of the dumps. The report stated that the local hoods had pre-empted the dumps to a certain extent, even holding nightly orgies there.

It is not surprising that Danger Town produced great boxers. In 1889, the year after McGuinness' birth, a Danger Town boxer named Jake Kilrain lost the last bear knuckle heavy championship bout to the legendary champion John L. Sullivan in a fifty-round affair outdoors, in nearly hundred-degree Mississippi heat, with an equal amount of humidity. The bout was well into its third hour when Kilrain's seconds, fearing one more round would kill him, threw in the towel. Another local boxer, William Dacey, lost a close bout to one of nine boxers never defeated in the ring: Williamsburg's legendary lightweight champion Jack McAuliffe. It is not surprising Pete followed them into the boxing ring.

As rough as the Danger Town hoodlums were, Officer Patrick Cusack was tougher. A barrel-chested, bear of a man, the officer was tougher than the toughest member of any Danger Town gang. He would stride right into a group of four or five gangsters and lay down the law. Once he was ordered to arrest one of the most feared gang members. Other cops were afraid, but not Cusack who walked calmly into their midst, told the leader he was under arrest and cuffed the man. No one in the gang dared start up with Cusack. The officer became a hero to McGuinness and the other boys in the area.

It was not thugs, gangs or robbery that was the scariest part of living in Danger town. It was the very real fear of fire. In such a heavily industrial area, fire was an ever-present danger. Years later, when McGuinness was trying to save the local Greenpoint to Manhattan ferry from being closed, he harkened back to the fears he and his neighbors must have felt in growing up in such a tinderbox. He said that the ferries would be the only means of escape from Greenpoint, in the main a community of frame buildings, in the event of fire. "Listen, pal," he told Mayor John P. O'Brien, "if somebody set fire to Greenpoint and them old boats weren't there, we'd all be roasted alive."

In Pete's childhood the fire tower, located behind the police station on the corner of Manhattan and Greenpoint Avenues, was very important. The clanging of the fire gong brought fear into the hearts of Greenpoint and locals heard the sound all too often. The Greenpoint-Williamsburg area was the most dangerous assignment for firemen in the city and there were far more fire houses there than other areas because of the high risk of a conflagration. The fact that many of the houses were attached wooden frame structures only added to the fear of fire. Two Eagle street businesses went up in flames in Pete's childhood. The Tannery at #22 was destroyed by fire on March 18, 1891 and the plant of the *Eagle Box Company* burned on March 17, 1893. One local fire during his childhood took the lives of seven children and consumed fifteen homes.

The local firemen were authentic heroes who continually risked their lives fighting fires. Greenpointers of Pete's era looked back on their childhood and recalled numerous scary neighborhood fires. The two Astral Oil fires were especially large because the huge oil tanks on the North Twelfth Street property fed the flames. One of the Astral fires took forty-eight hours of continuous fire fighting to extinguish and Greenpointers sat up all night watching the sky illuminated by the fire, worrying that the wind would change direction and blow the flames towards the area, consuming all the residences in its path. Luckily, the wind continued to blow east, away from residences.

The second fire at Pratt's oil works, October 11, 1888, was a sad one for the Greenpoint Avenue Fire Company. It was at this fire that Foreman Joseph J. McCormick, Firemen James Henry McElroy and Henry Helen were terribly burned by the explosion of a naphtha tank on the dock. McCormick was burned about the face, head and arms, and his hands were so severely burned that he never recovered use of them. McElroy's face and hands remained scared for life from the severe burns he received. The company was almost wiped out in a single fire in 1891 at the huge Palmer bagging factory in Williamsburg when the walls collapsed, nearly killing the company. The company's fire engine was crushed by the falling walls and destroyed.

Sugar refining employed many locals, but also caused huge fires because inflammable gases created in the refining process often ignited. The massive Havemayer plant in Williamsburg burned to the ground shortly before Pete's birth and the Havemayer plant in Greenpoint also went up in flames.

The most terrifying fire in Greenpoint history happened in McGuinness' first year on the Board of Aldermen, on September 13, 1919, a huge fire threatened to engulf the entire neighborhood in flames. The fire at the

Sone and Fleming oil works on Kingsland Avenue was one of the largest and most dangerous fires in Brooklyn history, leading to millions of dollars in damage and the evacuation of hundreds of residents. Many Greenpointers again feared being burned to death. Fires were common at the works, but the fire was not supposed to happen. The firm was well aware of the danger of such a fire and had installed a special pump to douse oil fires with steam. However, the explosion that started the fire was so strong it disabled the steam system and the yard, with a hundred huge oil and Naphtha tanks, lay defenseless.

The fire started in the afternoon when a fifty-five thousand gallon gas tank exploded. Five minutes later, the flames had spread to three other tanks. A fire alarm was sounded—as was a second, third and fourth, but the fire was so huge and dangerous that a borough-wide alarm went out. The fire soon engulfed the company's four-story office building on the site. Soon four hundred seventy-five fire fighters were battling the flames along with nine fireboats. However, because the fire had so much flammable liquid, it posed a special danger.

Civilians had to be evacuated and seven hundred females who worked in a local dye factory were evacuated to safety. Hundreds of tenement dwellers in the area around Kingsland and Norman Avenues also had to be evacuated. Many of them were Italian and Polish and their limited ability to communicate in English only added to their fear. In the rush to escape the flames children were trampled and one young Polish boy was seriously injured.

By about four-thirty the situation looked hopeless, with a hundred tanks on the site all in danger of exploding. Soon the fire had jumped the creek and burned a candle factory in Long Island City. Quickly the flames engulfed the Standard Oil works in Long Island City, even igniting the bridge connecting Long Island City and Greenpoint. All available fire fighters in the city eventually had to be called, along with all the available equipment.

The fire was so huge that it could be seen twenty miles away and continued to burn for a week. McGuinness summarized what a lot of people felt about the fire when he stated, "Nothing but Newtown Creek, the fire-boats and providence prevented the fire from wiping out of the entire district." When McGuinness realized that the local political machine was doing nothing to prevent the next big oil fire, it increased his conviction that he had to drive the machine out of power and help establish an honest, responsive government.

Chapter Ten: McCarren's Machine

McGuinness' political career began at the precocious age of eight during William Jennings Bryan 1896 presidential campaign. A year earlier McGuinness had already learned the names of all his neighbors. A natural at politics with a prodigious memory for names and faces and a hugely extroverted personality, McGuinness years later reflected back on his childhood love of politics. He said, "I knew I liked that kind of work the best," and added, "I was always a great one for anything that had to do with people."

Mr. Frank Cantwell, a local ward captain in the Jefferson Democratic Club, recognized that the eight-year-old McGuinness could turn out the vote as well as any adult. On election day one of his Ward captains was absent, threatening to lower his tally of votes, so he turned to McGuinness, giving him a slip of paper with the names of voters who had not cast their ballots yet. Cantwell told

Pete, "Go see 'em to come out and vote." Pete produced an amazing thirty or forty votes and the Jefferson Club took note. McGuinness was paid a dollar and rewarded with the position of errand boy. He joined the Jefferson Club as a ward healer in every election, turning out voters. The Local District Leader, John Carpenter, took note of the budding young politician and predicted a bright future for the lad.

The Jefferson Club was only one of fifteen or so Democratic clubs in staunchly Democratic Greenpoint. The neighborhood was hyper-political and gained a reputation for fiercely contested local elections. Street corner oratory was common in Pete's childhood, but Greenpoint politics was far from genteel. Politicians were pelted with rotten fruit or vegetables. Soaked loaves of bread were hurled from rooftops. Politicians often shouted down their opponents. Fisticuffs between bands of supporters were not uncommon. Such a rough and tumble environment was perfect for the physically intimidating McGuinness, who possessed a booming voice and a sharp wit.

Many of the clubs described themselves as "regular" Democratic clubs and the term requires some explanation. The goal of elections was not only for the candidates to win, but also for the spoil system to reward the most faithful supporters of the winning candidate with political jobs or a host of other favors. Fractiousness that could result in a third candidate challenging the party's choice could prove fatal to victory at the polls and to loyal Democrats seeking jobs. The party needed unity in order to achieve victory. Hence once a candidate was chosen, the loser's backers were expected to become regular Democrats and support the nominee, however distasteful he might have been.

Betty Smith, the author of the famous novel *"A Tree Grows in Brooklyn"* and a contemporary of McGuinness, described how the Democratic machine functioned on its most basic level. She imagined a conversation between the protagonist's father Johnny, a regular Democrat, and his wife in which Johnny explained how the party pays back its support. Smith created a typical conversation Brooklyn voters would have had about Tammany Hall, the corrupt, but powerful Manhattan political machine that was intent on grabbing power in Brooklyn. The conversation is an insight into how the machine functioned and why people supported it, despite its corruption.

Francie's father Johnny, like McGuinness, was an Irish-American Brooklyn Democrat who debated the pluses and minuses of the Tammany machine with his skeptical wife, who as a female still could not vote at the turn of the century. Johnny said, "By and large the party does a lot of good for the people." He continued, "All they want is a vote from the man of the family and look what they give him in exchange."

His wife skeptically asked what and he replied. "Well you need advice on a legal matter. You don't go to a lawyer. Just ask your assemblyman." He added, "They may be dumb in many ways, but they know the city's statutes backwards and forwards." Johnny continued, "Take Civil Service. They know when the examination for cops, firemen or letter carriers are coming up. They'll always put a voter wise if interested."

The woman recalled that one of the neighbors took the test without getting a job. Johnnie answered, "Ah, that's because he is a Republican. If he was a Democrat, they'd take his name and put it at the top of the list. I heard about a teacher who wanted to be transferred to another school. Tammany fixed it up."

Johnny continued, "Look at all the jobs they get for voters. You know how they get them, don't you? They inspect a factory and overlook the fact that they're violating the factory laws. Naturally, the boss pays back by letting them know when they need men and Tammany gets the credit for finding the jobs."

Johnny added, "A man has relatives in the old country but he can't get them over here on account of a lot of red tape. Well Tammany can fix that up. Sure they get them foreigners here and see to it that they start in on their citizenship papers and then tell them that they must vote the Democratic ticket or go back where they came from."

Johnny finished up explaining how Tammany helped the poor: "No matter what you say, Tammany is good to the poor people. Say a man's been sick and can't pay his rent. Do you think the organization would let the landlord dispossess him? No sir. Not if he is a Democrat."

His wife disputed his claims and replied, hinting that women would soon get the right to vote: "For what Tammany gives to the people it takes from them double. You wait until us women vote. You don't believe we will. The day will come; mark my words. We'll put all those crooked politicians where they belong—behind iron bars."

When the eight-year-old McGuinness started knocking on doors, the man at the top of the local Democratic hierarchy was State Senator Patrick McCarren, a hero to the young McGuinness. McCarren was a poor local Irish-American who also never had the chance to attend high school. He began life as an apprentice cooper, making barrels for the local sugar mill, but ambition led him into Democratic politics. At first, he ran as an outsider against the party designee and was trounced, but the local machine saw McCarren had the makings of a future leader. They co-opted him and eventually he was asked by the party to serve in the assembly. At the time, corrupt Democratic boss Hugh McLaughlin ran all of Brooklyn, becoming a millionaire through graft and corruption. Boss McLaughlin, like McCarren, was a working-class, first-generation Irish-American who used the party to rise to a position of power. Quickly, McCarren became one of his trusted lieutenants, proving his loyalty to McLaughlin.

McLaughlin quickly saw that McCarren, a very talented state assemblyman, was gifted at getting bills signed into law, but more importantly in blocking bills that could hurt McLaughlin's interests. McCarren was such an able legislator that the boss decided that he belonged in the state senate, not in the legislature.

McCarren soon became one of the most powerful Albany senators. A Machiavellian figure and an adept dealmaker, McCarren had fewer ideological barriers and still fewer moral scruples about cutting deals that would help corporate interests. He became one of the first corporate lobbyists in American history, amassing a fortune helping the very industries that stopped his constituents from unionizing and exploited them through forming cartels to jack up prices and restrict competition. The corporations that McCarren most vigorously defended were the enemies of his constituents: the Standard Oil Trust, which was destroying Newtown Creek, and the Sugar Trust, which overcharged for sugar while paying local workers starvation wages.

McCarren protected these big businesses, yet he was such an adept politician and kept the people so ignorant of his machinations that they supported him. When campaign time came corporate money was spent liberally. Local bars bought free drinks in return for votes and local longshoreman were paid handsomely to make sure that McCarren's opponents were physically intimidated. McCarren drew his staunchest support from Irish-Americans like the McGuinness family. They were proud that one of their own had made it, and McCarren trumpeted his humble local working class Irish-American origins.

McCarren succeeded not only in hoodwinking the voters and in gaining re-election, but also in bringing home the legislative bacon. Thanks to McCarren, North Brooklyn got the Williamsburg Bridge in 1903, and in the same year McCarren secured for the area the park that would bear his name after his death. Years later, as a young City Alderman, McGuinness made an impassioned speech in a failed effort to have the Williamsburg Bridge renamed the McCarren Bridge. McGuinness remained blissfully unaware that his hero was as much of a corporate puppet as any Republican.

By 1903, the City of Brooklyn had merged with Manhattan to form a city of five boroughs. McLaughlin was too old to adapt to the new reality of sharing power with Manhattan. The aged McLaughlin opposed two of the candidates Manhattan's Tammany Hall Democratic machine had nominated, violating the principal of regularity by refusing to support them. McCarren pleaded with the old boss to relent, but McLaughlin remained steadfast, so McCarren led a revolt against McLaughlin, deposed him and became leader of the Brooklyn Democrats. North Brooklyn rejoiced because now their local leader was also master of all Brooklyn. However, Tammany Hall had aspirations of controlling all of New York, just like it controlled Manhattan, and sought to crush McCarren and Brooklyn's political independence. McCarren defied Tammany Hall, saying that Brooklyn would not submit to its tyranny, while coining a famous phrase about the symbol of Tammany, the tiger: "The tiger shall not cross the (Brooklyn) bridge."

Tammany tested the solidarity of Brooklyn Democrats by getting a number of Brooklyn politicians to side with it and challenge McCarren and his slate of supporters. Despite tremendous pressure, Brooklyn stayed loyal to McCarren, whose candidates defeated Tammany's in local party elections. No place was more loyal to McCarren than Greenpoint, which was handsomely rewarded for its "regularity." Years later McGuinness named the political club he formed "The Greenpoint People's Regular Democratic Club," in all likelihood recalling the fight McCarren had in keeping political autonomy for Brooklyn. McCarren died in 1909 at age sixty at the height of his power when McGuinness was just twenty-one years old. Leadership of the Brooklyn Democrats would pass to a man who would turn his back on all McCarren fought for and pledge his loyalty to Tammany. His name was John McCooey who, years later, would become a McGuinness' enemy.

Chapter Eleven: The Fourteen McGuinnesses

McGuinness was never more ebullient and witty than on October 12, 1931 while testifying before the Hofstadter Commission, investigating corruption in New York City. On the witness stand Judge Seabury asked McGuinness how he was able to wrest the position of Democratic District Leader away from James McQuade, whose extended family included thirty-three relatives in the district. McGuinness lifted his head proudly and told the court about his own large family—"You can tell the world judge, there are fourteen McGuinesses."

The large McGuinness family was not unusual in Greenpoint. Greenpoint was growing more Catholic in the late 1880's as many Protestants left the area, replaced by large Catholic families like the McGuinness clan. The McGuinnesses were in many ways typical working-class New Yorkers. They were Irish-Americans, and in the 1880s forty percent of new Yorkers were either Irish, or had Irish extraction.

McGuinness was born in a house that still stands: 132 Eagle Street. The house, a small wooden frame structure set back off the street, probably was built even before the street was surveyed. Conditions must have been very cramped for sixteen people in such a tiny house, and none of Pete's sisters weighed under a hundred and fifty pounds and his brothers all weighed over two hundred pounds, but McGuinness retained a lifelong affection for his siblings. Many of them lived locally and his brother George became one of his most trusted advisors.

McGuinness was named for his father, Peter McGuinness Sr., but father and son did not get along well. When the elder McGuinness died at age seventy-four in 1926, he wrote in his last will and testament: "Some of my children have helped me and others have done nothing for me." McGuinness' father left $20,000—a considerable sum at that time, especially for a man who raised fourteen children. Pete, though, was one of the children cut off in the will. McGuinness, in an *Eagle* article about his father's will, stated that he had gotten all he wanted from his father during his lifetime and that he had helped him financially in his campaigns. It seems his father was ashamed of having a politician in the family. He had wanted Peter to follow in his footsteps as a brass polisher. "To the old gentleman," McGuinness said, "there was no job in the world as good as brass polishing. I never seen it that way."

McGuinness' father was born in New Jersey, but moved to Greenpoint in the decade of Peter's birth. McGuinness Sr. was a parishioner of St. Anthony of Padua and a practicing Catholic. We know little else about him. One thing that was very unusual for a working-class Irish-American—Alderman McGuinness never touched alcohol. McGuinness promised that he would have his first ever drink when Mayor Walker granted him a bridge across Newtown Creek, but reneged on his promise. Being tea-total was quite out of the ordinary for a working-class Greenpoint boy. Maybe Pete's father was an abusive drinker or there was another cause, but his abstinence certainly set Pete apart from his peers.

We also know little about his mother, Kate McGuinness. Train accidents played a horrible role in her life. Trains mangled two of her brothers, and her oldest son William was also tragically hit and killed by a train during a baseball game while visiting her family in New Jersey in 1903. We can only speculate how the fifteen-year-old McGuinness was affected by the death of his older brother, but perhaps the accident led years later to his getting two pieces of legislation passed into law: the first, a citywide speed limit and the other shutting off crowded streets to vehicles in summer so kids could play safely.

Evidently, Mrs. McGuinness was also a jealous woman. In 1892, when Pete was four, she hired a Ms. Kiesling to do wash as a temporary laundress. She noted, or imagined, a fondness by her husband for the laundress and in an apparent fit of jealousy, Mrs. McGuinness boxed the ear of the laundress' little boy, Charlie, for which she was arrested. Justice Watson had the unenviable task of judging the case against Mrs. McGuinness, and the anger of the two women poisoned his courtroom. He acquitted Mrs. McGuinness, but noted, "Had I the power I would send one of you to live in Hoboken and the other in Greenpoint. That would be better than letting you both live in the same house."

It must have been a huge burden on McGuinness' family to make ends meet with so many children. Peter, keenly aware of the financial challenges the family faced, worked at odd jobs in the neighborhood from age five or six. He ran errands for storekeepers, carried growlers of beer for workingmen, and sold the eggs of some hens he kept in the back yard. He also sold the local newspaper *The Greenpoint Weekly Star*, so by the time he was 10, McGuinness was well known throughout Greenpoint. "I was pals with the whole town," he said.

Young Greenpoint boys were very social, often forming their own social clubs. One group of boys older than McGuinness had formed an organization called "The

Rinky Dinks" in about 1900. The club hosted carnivals and balls as well as having a lot of political influence. On weekends the young McGuinness served as the standard-bearer for the group's marching society. "The Rinks were a lot of young fellows around the Point," he said. "All of them was keeping company with girls, and the girls marched with them. Nobody wanted to leave his young lady friend to carry the flag, so they hired me to do it." These parades were often held at night with torches and banners that announced events that the group was hosting. These marches were riotous affairs that McGuinness recalled with fondness. McGuinness was paid a quarter to carry the group's standard through the area.

Years later, McGuinness told an anecdote about a Rinky Dinks affair. One night the Rinky Dinks were indiscrete enough to enter a hall where another group was having a cotillion. The offended group targeted McGuinness with bottles and chairs and grabbed him. Suddenly, he felt himself being lifted off the ground and thrown bodily out the window. Luckily for Greenpoint, the window was only five feet above the alley and McGuinness was unhurt. The next day he proudly went and collected his quarter.

Perhaps Peter and his brothers inherited their fighting spirit and boxing skills from their mother. One thing is certain: the McGuinness boys were scrappers who enjoyed a good fistfight. Years later, an aged Greenpointer recalled in *The Brooklyn Daily Eagle* the fear that he had walking by the McGuinness house because one risked getting a beating from one of the McGuinness brothers.

Once, during Peter's childhood, one of the McGuinness brothers began an altercation with a young Scottish immigrant boy named John MacCrate who had just moved onto the block. It would be the unusual start to a lifelong friendship between MacCrate and McGuinness. MacCrate became a revered local figure, known all around Greenpoint as Scotty. Forty-five years later, McGuinness recalled, "Scotty could fight like it was nobody's business." MacCrate later reflected on Pete's character saying, "His leadership qualities were apparent as a boy and although he was physically capable of handling anyone, he was a pacifier." The fact that McGuinness was a Catholic Democrat and MacCrate a Protestant Republican did not diminish the friendship the two had for one another. The scrappy Scot's father arrived in Brooklyn to toil as a worker in the Brooklyn Navy Yard and when he had saved up enough he sent for his family to come and join him in the new world. McGuinness and MacCrate became best friends, despite their differences.

They both attended P.S. 31 on DuPont Street, but Scotty proved to be the far better student. The actions of MacCrate's teacher, Isabel Ennis, changed Scotty's life forever. In those days, few working class children, like Scotty and McGuinness, attended high school, and at the end of eighth grade Scotty informed his favorite teacher that he was dropping out of school. Horrified because MacCarate had a first-rate mind, Ennis accompanied MacCarate home, sat down with his parents and pleaded with them to let Scotty continue his education. MacCarate was allowed to go to night school, and eventually went to college and even law school, thanks to this concerned teacher.

Contemporaries of MacCrate and McGuinness recalled with fondness political debates the two would have during their twenties in a Manhattan Avenue coffee shop. McGuinness argued for the Democrats, while MacCrate supported the Republicans. Pete was not MacCarate's intellectual equal, and McGuinness grew more and more animated as the debates swung in MacCarate's favor. McGuinness raised his hands and gesticulated wildly, much to the delight of the audience, who agreed with him, but sided with MacCrate, just to enjoy the spectacle of McGuinness' anger and frustration.

Greenpoint residents had a working-class solidarity that united them and there was a strong sense of equality, but the community also had its celebrities.

Chapter Twelve: The Celebrities of Greenpoint

McGuinness' Greenpoint, with a strong sense of community pride and solidarity that transcended social class, was more like a small town than an urban area. The working class lived in tenements or framed houses, while the entrepreneurs and professionals lived nearby in elegant homes on Kent or Milton Street. The McGuinness brothers played and prayed with everyone, even millionaires, and Peter personally knew most of the local celebrities.

The richest families in Greenpoint were the two branches of the ancestral Meserole family, who had made fortunes in real estate, manufacture and banking. Adrian Meserole, of the Southern branch, lived on Lorimer Street, becoming a real estate mogul and millionaire. Mary Meserole, part of the northern branch, married Neziah Bliss, the rich patriarch of Greenpoint. Their millionaire son, Archibald Bliss, represented the area in Congress, but was later defeated in his bid to become mayor of Brooklyn.

One of the richest men in Greenpoint was millionaire Thomas Smith, the founder of the Union Porcelain Works on Eckford Street. His house still stands on Milton Street and has become the Reformed Church. Smith embodied the can-do spirit that Greenpointers took pride in. He succeeded in creating the first hard porcelain factory in the United States, despite having no prior experience. Smith's factory produced pieces that won national competitions and are still prized possessions of museums around the country.

If money gained millionaires respect, then religious leaders were also greatly respected, none more than Rev. Patrick O'Hare, McGuinness' parish pastor at St. Anthony of Padua Roman Catholic Church. A universally loved, but feared figure, the pastor was known as "The Mayor of Greenpoint." O'Hare inherited a demoralized and bickering flock in the 1880's, but threw himself into solving the parish's problems, the first of which was lack of money. A dynamic preacher, he exhorted his congregation to contribute money, and the parish quickly liquidated its large debt. Within a year, he had found a rich patron to fund renovation of the deteriorating interior, transforming the church's interior into a thing of amazing beauty.

As tough of any Greenpoint boxer, O'Hare welded his

flock into a spiritual community. He raised the funds to rebuild the parish school. When local stores placed scantily clad manikins in shop windows, he successfully pressured the storeowners to remove them. He formed the Order of the Cross, which dealt with the rampant local alcohol problem. O'Hare threatened saloon owners who violated liquor laws and they reluctantly complied with the law rather than face O'Hare's wrath. He even visited the local vaudeville theaters to ensure decency. When he deemed an act unwholesome, theater owners often removed it, fearing O'Hare's censure. One star, though, was too big to ban, the legendary vaudeville temptress and singer Eva Tanguey, whose show he forbid his parishioners from going to see. She taunted him from the stage singing, "Father O'Hare, I don't care." O'Hare had inherited a congregation of several hundred, but helped it grow to several thousand.

In 1895, during the bitter trolley strike, O'Hare won the lasting love of his congregation. Many parishioners were trolley operators employed by the Brooklyn City Railroad Company. In the early 1890s, the stockholders of the BCRC reorganized a new company in Virginia, not subject to New York regulations. The stockholders had found a means of reaping large profits, and at the same time evading New York State labor laws.

Many trolley operators were the neighbors of the McGuinness family who had grievances with the trolley company, believing they deserved better wages now that the newly electrified trolley system was more demanding work. However, the major conflict between labor and management was the 10-hour workday. New York State law limited workers to no more than 10 hours in a 12-hour period. The trolley men believed that the 10 hours included meals and time spent waiting for their trolleys at the train depot. The company, though, did not intend to pay workers for any time not spent actually running the trolleys.

The trolley company rejected the workers' demands. The union relented on the pay raise, but would not budge on the 10-hour day, and the union's executive board voted to endorse a citywide strike. Five thousand workers all over Brooklyn went on strike, paralyzing the borough's trolley system. Although the first day of the strike was peaceful, the situation quickly deteriorated and violence began to occur when the company hired scab workers, believing that replacing the striking workers quickly would enable the company to break the strike. All Greenpoint supported the strikers. For days violence ruled Greenpoint, the center of worker rebellion. Wires were cut and trolley windows were smashed. The company dared not try and move its cars at first.

The small, outnumbered local police force could do little, and many cops openly sided with the strikers. On January 24, 1895, there was a riot as the company tried to take the cars along Manhattan Avenue. A huge crowd formed at the Box Street depot and the police rushed the menacing crowd with clubs drawn. Trolley windows were smashed with stones. Large crowds on Manhattan Avenue surrounded a subsequent car trying to move southward, and members of the crowd berated the scab motormen, while pulling their sleeves.

Fr. O'Hare ventured out onto Manhattan Avenue to support the strikers, but the *Daily Eagle* condemned the priest, claiming that he supported violence. The strikers eventually lost, returning to work without winning any of their demands, but O'Hare's support of the strikers gained him the lifelong affection of his congregation. O'Hare's solidarity with the strikers must have had a profound effect on the seven-year-old McGuiness. He once said, "The people of Greenpoint have lived there all their lives and they stick together."

The Baptist community was led by Reverend David Hughes, the pastor of the Union Baptist Church on Noble Street, a fire and brimstone preacher with a thousand children in the Sunday school and a huge flock. However, it was not Reverend Hughes, but his brilliant son Charles Evans Hughes, who would make history. Hughes Sr. raised his only son to become a minister, but, perhaps revolted by the stifling religious conservatism of the family, his son chose not to study religion and became a highly successful corporate lawyer instead, much to the dismay of his father and mother.

Hughes might have continued quietly practicing corporate law, but his sense of civic duty led him to head New York State commissions investigating abuse in the insurance industry and electricity monopoly. His revelations about corruption and consumer abuse shocked New York State, while showing conclusively that policyholders were being overcharged. They also revealed a host of corrupt alliances between the companies and politicians, exposing bribery, graft, and corruption among the state's politicians.

Cementing his reputation as a foe of corruption, the investigation led reformers to clamor for Hughes to run for governor. Rapidly, he became the darling of the state's papers, and suddenly Hughes became the leading Republican reform candidate for governor and gained the backing of President Teddy Roosevelt. Hughes got the Republican nomination and won the general election for Governor in 1907, hoping to wipe out corruption and empower the voters. Hughes would go on to serve as secretary of state, governor and unsuccessful Republican nominee for President in 1916. However, it was on the Supreme Court where he shone brightest. He was chosen chief justice of the highest court and is considered one of the greatest chief justices in history.

Many people, however, could not believe that the eminent Supreme Court chief justice had grown up in working class Greenpoint. McGuinness, though, with his huge memory for names and faces, recalled that Hughes as a boy had punched his uncle in the nose after a baseball diamond argument. In 1943, Robert Moses, the famed power broker of New York City, bet McGuinness that Hughes had never lived in Greenpoint. He lost and the controversy made its way into *The New York Times*: On Mr. Moses' personal stationary was a short note addressed "Dear Pete," it said: "I thought you might be interested in the attached letter from Justice Hughes. You win." It read:

> My home was in Greenpoint for about nine and a half years—from October, 1874, to May, 1884—while my father was pastor of the Union Avenue (now Manhattan Avenue) Baptist Church," Justice Hughes wrote. "It is fair to add that I was not exposed to the beneficial atmosphere of Green-

> point for as long a time as this might indicate. I was away from home most of the time… But I had many good friends in Greenpoint and I cherish the memory of my association there.

McGuinness added gleefully, "Those (years in Greenpoint) were his formative years. If it wasn't for Greenpoint, he wouldn't be what he is today."

Hughes might have been the most important statesman to come out of Greenpoint, but the most popular person was a woman: the great Hollywood actress and sex symbol Mae West. At the height of McGuinness' fame, West was asked if she knew McGuinness, but she did not. If Mae did not know Pete, then her father, Battlin' Jack West, did. Both men were boxers who probably met at the Standard A.C. Boxing Club on Manhattan Avenue. West, a boxer since age eleven, fought his first boxing match as a featherweight, dreaming of becoming a bare-knuckles champion.

In the late 1880s, though, Jack found something more interesting than boxing, a buxom young Bavarian teenage beauty named Matilda Doelger—or as her friends called her, Tillie—a former corset and fashion model. Tillie arrived in Brooklyn in 1886, joining a large German community in Greenpoint. Jack swept her off her feet. They were both dreamers who defied the practical aspirations of their parents, Jack by boxing and Tillie through dreams of a theatrical career. In 1889, a year after Pete's birth, Battlin' Jack West and Tillie Doelger took their wedding vows before a Greenpoint minister. They lived out their dreams vicariously through their famous daughter Mae.

Jack and Mae adored each other, and with his backing Mae entered vaudeville at the precocious age of five, later becoming a star and ending up in Hollywood. Mrs. McGuinness said she was not among Mae West's greatest admirers, but she went anyway to honor local talent. "I guess she does that wiggling just to be comical," she said of West in one of her rare interviews.

What Fr. O'Hare and Rev. Hughes were to piety, the Barrison sisters were to scandal. Growing up on India Street, they were slightly older than Peter. It is not clear if Pete knew them personally, but he would have known about them, as they were the queens of Greenpoint scandal. The sisters—Lola, Sophia, Niger, Olga and Gertrude—were plump and uninhibited Danish immigrants who soon became vaudeville stars. They were cute, cheeky exhibitionists. Lola became an outstanding beauty, well-developed and temperamental. In 1890 she married a Broadway press agent—who engineered a tour that took them all over the world. They played Berlin for eight months, and they wowed the Folies-Bergere (to cries of "Vives les Americaines!"), with their innocent faces, schoolgirl costumes and suggestive songs.

They achieved notoriety, however, by ingenious use of double-entendres on stage. Berlin was particularly impressed with the number, "Meine Kleine Katz." The curtain rose a few feet, to show five frilly petticoats. "Would you like to see my pussy?" warbled the girls. The audience did, so the curtain continued to rise, as did the petticoats, until a fluffy black kitten was revealed peering our of each girl's knickers. A smitten French nobleman even committed suicide for love of Lola and they scandalized so many that they were eventually barred from re-entering Germany. They returned to the United States. The *Times* reviewer panned their performance and was deeply shocked by their revealing costumes and their risqué songs.

In 1896 *The Brooklyn Daily Eagle* dispatched a reporter to India Street to report on the wicked sisters. The sisters' names were in the paper because a different aristocrat had shot himself out of unrequited love for one of them. Even though the family was poor, the girls grew up proud, and evidently none of the sisters showed the least interest in Greenpoint boys, much to the local boys' chagrin. Some of the sour-grapes locals observed that the sisters "never had any use for the other people on the block" and had a "my mammy won't let me play with you attitude." They left Greenpoint for the world stage and stardom, never to return, but no locals ever forgot them or failed to gossip about their scandalous escapades.

Although the fourteen-year-old McGuinness loved Greenpoint, he left his neighborhood to work in Manhattan. He ended up in Manhattan's toughest and most colorful area, the Bowery, and it had a profound influence on him. Pete saw a lot of depravity there, but he would meet a benevolent Bowery machine politician who would inspire him to set up a similar political machine in Greenpoint.

Chapter Thirteen: The Bowery

At age fourteen, McGuinness graduated grammar school and went to work in Manhattan, while commuting home by ferry to Greenpoint. At first, McGuinness worked as an office boy, but it paid little. In 1902, Pete quickly left for more lucrative, but dangerous, work in the dive bars and seedy theaters of Manhattan's legendary Bowery. Decades later, a writer doing a piece for the *New Yorker* commented on the Bowery's effect, "Everything about McGuinness's speech and appearance suggests the old Bowery." Although McGuinness said he was never a Bowery Boy, his dress, his verbal expressions, manner of speech and his colorful persona all reminded people of the turn-of-the-century Bowery.

To many reformers the Bowery represented all that was wrong with America, but Americans had a lurid fascination with the area. The street became identified with vice, but also great entertainment. Alcoholism, opium abuse, homelessness and prostitution existed side by side with great shows. A Bowery writer, though, captured the despair of the place. Ignatz Leo Nascher's "*The Wretches of Povertyville*:" described its depravity, "Tis a wretched world, this underworld of Povertyville, where poverty begets vice, and vice begets crime, where virtue has its price, and conscience is stilled, then forgotten." It was also notorious with the police. Twenty-seven percent of all city arrests were made in the Bowery. Rape, murder, and robbery were common there. It was rightfully called, "the paradise of the criminal."

The Bowery, though, was also a place where a big, tough Greenpoint kid could thrive. McGuinness downplayed the crime in the area in his recollections saying, "There was some splendid people on the Bowery in them days,... but I never thought too much of the place. I'm a neighborhood man myself, and the Bowery wasn't really what you'd call a neighborhood. It wasn't so tough as they say, neither."

McGuinness was paid $5.00 a week, risking his life delivering Thomas Plunkett's celebrated cigars to the many notorious local saloons, clubs and theaters. They were not only the hangouts of gangsters, thieves, johns and prostitutes, but also the scenes of many robberies and murders. Gangs often controlled the saloons where criminals conducted business meetings openly, without fear. Perhaps the scenes he saw on the Bowery made him avoid drink. Years later he spoke of "Jesse James night-clubs," because the Bowery was notorious for places that literally robbed patrons.

Although the area was a hothouse for crime, it was also the birthplace of much of American popular culture. More respectable citizens ventured there for its many great shows. Tony Pastor's Theater, the first vaudeville theater, helped define American popular culture. Mae West channeled the Bowery into her persona when she told Cary Grant's mission worker to "Come up and see me sometime" in *She Done Him Wrong* (1933), her first big film, which recreated the gay '90s Bowery. Her stage and film partner, the iconic W.C. Fields, also performed on Bowery stages.

If the Bowery had great theater, the real-life characters McGuinness met were even more dramatic. He met Steve Brodie, who won fame supposedly by jumping off the Brooklyn Bridge. Another character was the Bowery icon Chuck Connors, who grew up tormenting the Chinese by pulling their pigtails, but eventually learned some Mandarin-earning him his nickname, the Mayor of Chinatown. As an adult Connors worked as a bouncer in a variety of Bowery dive bars, becoming well known as a tour guide for celebrities, prominent authors and even royalty. Connors' reputation as a friend of the Chinese made him a convincing guide to his danger-seeking clientele, who believed his identification of innocent passers-by as hatchet men. Connors also created bogus opium dens, where the "fiends" paid no attention to the tour groups passing through.

Tourists came to experience the Bowery's dangerous pleasure, which made it the destination for New York's thrill-seekers for more than a century. The very worst dive McGuinness went to was McGurk's Suicide Hall, the lowest rung for prostitutes, hence the suicide craze that gave it its name and its grisly allure for tourists. More than a dozen people took their lives in the place.

Most likely McGuinness met one of the most notorious figures of the Bowery, the gang leader Monk Eastman. Eastman was so crude in appearance that he could have modeled for the stereotypical cartoon crook. He had a bullet-shaped head, a broken nose, cauliflower ears, prominently throbbing veins, numerous knife scars, pendulous jowls, and a bull neck, and was usually seen wearing an undershirt, with a small derby perched on the back of his head of longish, unkempt hair, but always accompanied by his pigeons.

Eastman quickly earned notoriety for being a brawler

and as the premier neighborhood thug. He soon recruited his own gang, the Eastmans, who established a headquarters on Chrystie Street. Quickly embroiled in turf wars with rival gangs, the Eastmans engaged in a range of criminal activity from protection rackets, to organizing prostitution rings, to fixing elections that ensured "political" protection from Tammany Hall. Eastman's reputation as a lunatic earned him the job of "sheriff," or bouncer, at the New Irving Hall, a celebrated club on Broome Street. He patrolled the New Irving with a four-foot "locust," or police day-stick, in hand, on which he carved a notch for every head bashed. On the night he reached 49 notches, Eastman reportedly whacked an innocent bystander so as to make it an even 50.

The New Irving attracted the crème de la crème of New York's scum. Almost all the customers were either thieves or prostitutes. Monk was quite skilled at using brass knuckles to knock out unruly customers, but it was his proud boast that he took them off every time he had to quiet an obstreperous female. Early in his career, he inflicted so many injuries that ambulance drivers dubbed Bellevue's accident ward, "the Eastman Pavilion."

These pugilistic talents were noticed by Tammany Hall, and soon Monk and his gang of thugs were election day fixtures, voting for their candidates two, three, four or more times and suggesting to other voters it would be healthy for them to vote the same way. Such a valuable man as Monk made many powerful friends, and he was routinely released just as soon as he was arrested, leaving him free to attend to the business of his hood-for-hire operation, which efficiently offered head whackings or ear chewings for $15, stabbings for $25 and more serious forms of mayhem for $100.

McGuinness not only met hoods on the Bowery, but he also met Big Tim Sullivan, the Tammany Hall political boss who was called "the King of the Bowery." Years later McGuinness recalled the Bowery District Leader as "splendid," and Sullivan served a role model for McGuinness, who years later set up his own Greenpoint political machine, incorporating many of the features of the Sullivan's Bowery machine.

McGuinness admired Sullivan because they had much in common. Both men were Irish-Americans, reared in poverty who had little chance for formal education. They were powerful men who were almost exactly the same height and weight, and the two ward leaders were charismatic, generous, likable men who were natural leaders.

Sullivan, born in dire poverty to large family in a Bowery hovel in 1862 or 1863, always recalled the day when a teacher realizing that his shoes were little more than rags sent him to a Tammany ward boss who got him a decent pair of shoes. Although he rose out of poverty, he never forgot his humble origins and stressed that he was just like his impoverished constituents. Like McGuinness, he worked first as a newsboy, but by twenty-one he had bought his own saloon. When he knocked out a boxer physically abusing a woman on the street, he passed the test of courage that the gangs needed to consider him a leader. A feared gang called the Whyos used his saloon as a base and helped Sullivan to get elected to the Assembly by voting again and again as repeaters and by threatening voters for other candidates. Sullivan eventually was chosen by Tammany Hall to be the district leader of the Lower East Side, and soon Sullivan was crowned king of the area.

Sullivan understood one fact of political life in New York City perfectly well, grasping the concept that running the Bowery was a profession and his power depended on the perceived benefits of his constituents. He summed up the situation: "When you get down to brass tacks it's the work that does the business." Sullivan's machine might have been corrupt, but it served the people at a time when there was no safety net. The machine offered jobs, legal support, social events, fuel, food and even shelter if necessary: the emerging machine itself was a profession. Party leaders wanted three things: votes, spoils and power. Tammany Hall survived countless scandals because it did not merely take: it gave back to an impoverished community. These lessons were not lost on the young boy from Greenpoint.

One feature of the Sullivan machine McGuinness most likely brought back to Greenpoint: Christmas dinner. Sullivan reached into his own pocket to host Christmas dinner for literarily thousands of his poorest constituents. The constituents were not only fed, but the fathers were also given work boots and the children received toys. This same Christmas dinner with the gifts became a defining feature of McGuinness' rule in Greenpoint.

Sullivan owned a number of Bowery saloons and tightly controlled all the others in the area. He personally chose the staff in his saloons, for he knew that for the remaining local Irish the saloon was the de-facto social center and Sullivan political club. It was almost certainly in one of the local saloons that Sullivan met the young McGuinness delivering cigars. Perhaps McGuinness first dreamed of someday becoming political ruler of Greenpoint after meeting Sullivan.

There was, however, one huge difference: Sullivan was involved in graft. Gamblers, saloon owners and far shadier elements paid his machine for cover. McGuinness probably left the Bowery because its sordid vice and corruption revolted him. He was looking for a chance to return home. Years later he would set up a Tammany Hall style local machine, but it would avoid the graft that was a hallmark of Big Tim's machine in the Bowery.

There was another far more compelling reason McGuinness was eager to settle down in Greenpoint: love.

Chapter Fourteen: Orr's Lumber Yard

McGuinness could have stayed in Manhattan and built a career there, but romance brought him back to Greenpoint. McGuinness had already fallen in love with a local woman he would marry. In 1907, the nineteen-year-old McGuinness married eighteen-year-old Margaret Lyons and they would remain together for four decades until McGuinness' death. She was a large, attractive Irish-American woman who soon bore him a son: George. We know little else about her.

McGuinness needed to support his new family, so in 1908 he started work as a as a lumber handler at Orr's lumber Yard on Green and West Streets on Greenpoint's teeming waterfront. McGuinness would keep the job for a decade and he loved the work, explaining, "Working in a lumberyard is like being in a health resort all year long." He explained, "You're out there in God's good air all the day long, and from the smell of the different woods, you might as well be in a forest. And another thing you're in with the most splendid people. I never knew higher-class type men than lumber handlers."

Orr's was the oldest lumberyard in New York City, but it was only one of many. Greenpoint shipyards needed wood for the schooners they built, so Greenpoint had most of the city's lumberyards. In Pete's youth the sugar and oil industries also relied on wooden barrels to transport their products, so there were mountains of the staves that made barrels all over Greenpoint.

In the year of Pete's birth, 1888, a Greenpoint lumberyard owner, James Leary, gained international fame and made history when he successfully floated his Joggins raft to Whale Creek in Greenpoint from Joggins, Nova Scotia, a journey of seven hundred nautical miles. The 595-foot long wooden raft astonished locals with its size. It was 38 feet deep and the mass of logs was bound together with iron chains and steel wire and it was almost as solid as though it were the trunk of some giant tree. Leary used some of the timber for his shipyard, large amounts for his dock construction contracts, and the rest for sale at his timber yard. The raft safely arrived in Greenpoint to cheers, instantly making Leary rich.

Pete's job involved moving hundreds of pounds of lumber a day and the work built the already stocky McGuinness into a powerhouse, but his excellence in the lumber business was more than physical. He quickly became head tally clerk of Orr's Yard. The management respected his honesty, rapport with the men, intelligence and toughness. Pete successfully managed the massive inventories of the yard, but he also knew how to manage men. Once a ship was delivering a bad batch of wood. Pete refused to accept the bad wood, even though a dozen sailors threatened him. He quickly knocked out three of the startled group and lectured those still conscious on the need for honesty in business. He soon became chief stevedore in the yard, with responsibility to offload tons of lumber and supervisor of dozens of men. Pete was tough but fair, and a natural leader of men.

Most of the dockworkers were tough Irish Americans who often boxed in local clubs and sparred in bouts atop huge piles of wood or on barges in Newtown Creek to stop police interference. Pete, loud and outspoken with a charming gift for gab, soon became a rising figure in Lumber Handlers' Local 955 of the International Longshoremen's Association, but one incident cemented his rise in the union.

As a young dockworker, a conflict made Pete famous amongst the longshoremen and helped launch his future political career. The longshoreman's union was tied up with the Irish white hand mob and was notorious for corrupt union officials. McGuinness caught a pair of corrupt longshoremen union delegates in the act of splitting up hard-earned union dues for their own pleasure. He narrated:

> "It was at a meeting of the local in Germania Hall," Pete recounted. "I was in the Gents' Room. I was sitting down. These two delegates come in and start talking. They don't know no one is there. I'm a son of a bitch, they're divvying up one hundred thirty-two bucks they just took in dues. The sweats running down me back. I pull up me pants and go for them. I flang one of them through a glass panel door and knocked (out) the other cold. Then I marched them into the room where the Lumber Handlers was. Me and a friend made them empty their pockets on the table. They come up with a hundred and fifty. I made a motion we teach them a lesson by using the other eighteen for beer and bologna sandwiches for the whole local. Me friend seconded it, and it passed unanimous.

Before the meeting was adjourned for the beer and sandwiches, there was a purge of the Local 955 leadership, and McGuinness got the first of several union promotions. He said that his fight with the delegates was one of the very few serious fights he ever had. He explained, "We had fights almost every day, but they were just for fun. Besides, you had to do that to become boss in them days. The others figured that if they could lick me they could be boss theirselves. Most of the time we'd fight at lunch hour or after work. Everybody'd stand around and watch."

After the fights he began to practice his oratory, standing on a pile of lumber and giving the longshoremen all a talk or "a hot spiel" on the oppression of the Irish, liberty or even George Washington. The other longshoremen would say, "Bejesus, Peter, you're improving every day. Pretty soon we'll be after sending you to the board of aldermen." Their words would prove prophetic.

Pete kept his union card all his life and sometimes signed his name Peter J. McGuinness L.H. (Lumber Handler). Years later, at the start of the cold war, he told a group of reporters that he wished to make a suggestion on peacetime military training: "If they was to leave this conscription thing up to me, he said, "I'd have the boys putting in a couple of years in lumberyards. It builds up every muscle in your body. Lumber handlers are the toughest men on earth. Bejesus, if the Russians, or somebody, knew they'd be up against lumber handlers, they wouldn't start no trouble."

McGuinness Birthplace, 132 Eagle Street

The Monitor, 1861

Sullivan-Kilrain Fight

Monsignor O'Hare

Newtown Creek Around the Time of McGuinness' Birth

Newtown Creek in 1890's

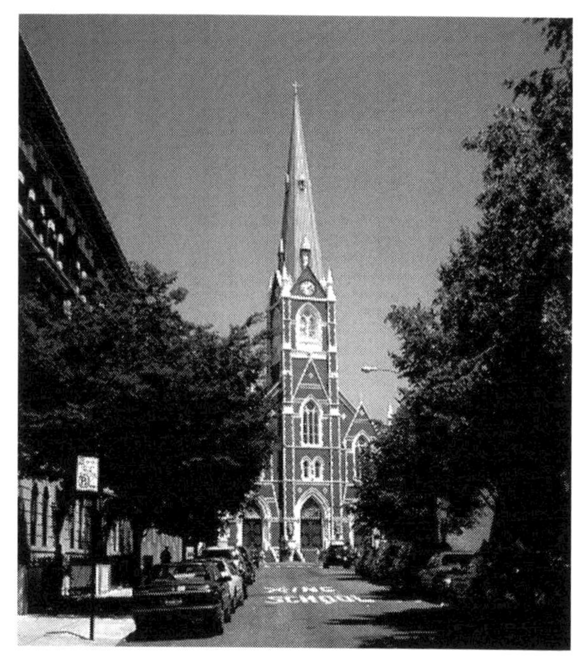

St. Anthony of Padua Church

Greenpoint Around 1900

A Greenpoint Fire Company

Oil Refineries in Greenpoint

Charles Evans Hughes

Pete's Wedding Photo

McGuinness with His Wife

Farm Gardens in McCarren Park during World War I

McGuinness with John MacCrate

McGuinness with Supporters During Early Campaign

McGuinness as a Young Alderman

McGuinness helped raise funds for this World War I Monument in McGolrick Park

McGuinness Pitching for Aldermen

McGuinness Playing Baseball for Aldermen

James McQuade

Sketch of McGuinness

McGuinness at Park Opening 1924

Opening of McCarren Park Pool 1935

Anti- McGuinness Cartoon

Al Smith's Picture Defaced

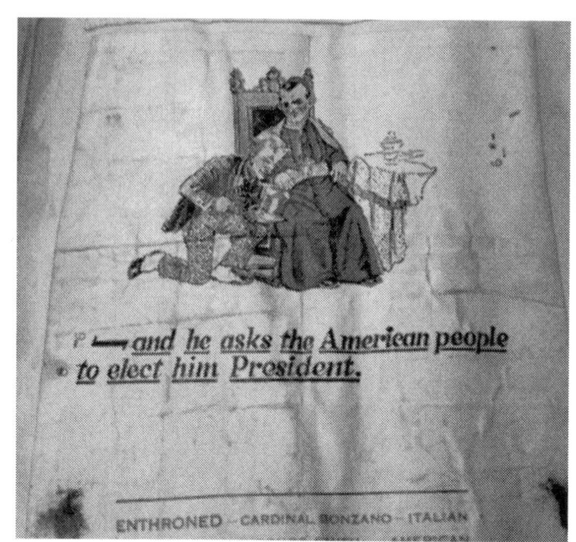

—and he asks the American people
to elect him President.
ENTHRONED – CARDINAL BONZANO – ITALIAN

Anti-Catholic Campaign Material 1928

McGuinness' New Club at
119 Norman Avenue

McGuinness' Home,
631 Leonard Street

McGuinness at Opening
of the Subway in 1933

Opening of the Crosstown Subway 1933

Civic Virtue Statue

McGuinness at 1936 Democratic National Convention

McGuinness with Aldermen

McGuinness at a Democratic Function

McGuinness in the 1930's

McGuinness at
McCarren Park Pool

Oakland Street, Which Became McGuinness Boulevard

McGuinness' Funeral 1948

Chapter Fifteen: The Native Borns

In 1928, McGuinness' sworn enemy, Registrar James McQuade, was still engaged in his vengeful feud with McGuinness. Never forgiving McGuinness for taking away his position as Democratic District Leader, McQuade was looking for an attack on McGuinness. He decided to play the Polish card against McGuinness, and recalled for the newspapers a long-forgotten incident from Pete's youth. He alleged that McGuinness had created an anti-immigrant secret society before the First World War in 1912 called the "Native Borns" to drive the Poles out of Greenpoint.

On March 20, 1928, *The Brooklyn Daily Eagle* published an article alleging that McGuinness had founded the xenophobic organization years earlier. McQuade stated, "McGuinness started the society to drive the Poles out of Greenpoint. He never thought at the time that he would someday be in politics." He also spread the rumor that his rival had told Polish people he did not need them and that they could go to hell.

McGuinness realized that his archenemy had hit upon an explosive issue and his failure to respond forcefully could mean losing the decisive local Polish vote. McGuinness immediately responded, not by denying his membership in the Native Borns, but by refuting the charge that the Native Borns were xenophobic. He said that the group was just the crew at the St. Edwards Hotel on Manhattan Avenue and that it only played poker and pinochle. McGuinness shot back, "If McQuade knew his onions, he would know that half the fellows in it were Polish." McGuinness counterclaimed not only that McQuade himself was a member of the nativist group, but also that he "nearly broke his neck to get into the Native Borns."

McQuade responded to the counter-charges by calling the district leader a liar and denying the charge that he was a member of the club. He said, "As far as I am concerned I would not join it because my parents came from the Emerald Isle and I wanted to see everyone, native born or otherwise, make a living in this country and have happy and prosperous homes."

The conflict surrounding the Native Borns highlighted the growing prominence of the large Polish community in local politics. One figure put the combined Russian and Polish population of Greenpoint at eighty percent on the eve of World War I. The terrible air pollution and stench of the area had driven many locally born people away and Slavic people quickly replaced them. The Poles had first come to the area before McGuinness' birth, attracted by the many factory jobs that required no English language skills. Many Polish women worked making ropes in the American Manufacturing Company on West Street and the men labored in the Havemayer Sugar Refinery on Commercial Street.

The Havemayer family, German-American sugar barons, ran huge North Brooklyn sugar refineries and dominated American sugar production, employing thousands of local Poles. Together with other Brooklyn sugar makers they secretly formed a cartel in 1887, based on the Standard Oil model, to regulate price and production, while quietly making themselves vast fortunes. For years Henry Havemayer set the price of sugar in most of the United States, but never shared his vast profits with his workers, fiercely resisting the unionization of his plants. Sugar profits funded his massive art collection, which was the largest donation the Metropolitan Museum of Art ever received. Havemayer died in 1907, in part because of stress brought on by revelations that his corporation had secretly inserted springs into the scales, under weighing raw sugar for tariffs and cheating the Federal Government out of millions of tax dollars. At first, many of the workers were fellow German-Americans, but the horrific conditions and low pay drove them out of the local mills. There were a series of unsuccessful, sometimes violent, strikes to improve pay and conditions. Poles who had recently emigrated from Eastern Europe unwittingly served in the sugar mills as strikebreakers, quickly replacing the German-American workers. Greenpoint soon became one of the world's largest Polish communities outside of Poland.

The Poles came here escaping desperate rural poverty at home. Often illiterate, many had a hard time learning English and adapting. In 1900, *The Brooklyn Daily Eagle* printed an expose on the sugar industry revealing the naked prejudice against the Poles in Brooklyn: "The Christian Pole is dull, not very shrewd or progressive, not as invariably honest as a bank manager, but he is faithful to his family, gets drunk principally at weddings, funerals and christenings, hence he likes to have these things happen as often as possible; lives miserably in order to save money and is a good workman at any job that does not require much skill or intellect." The writer added, "Our newly acquired Polacks may awaken to the importance of being represented in the board of alderman a little later, but at present they would rather have a few gallons of whiskey than an office." It continued:

> That the Pole is feared by the German and the Irish is obvious. You do not have to talk long with the people in the sugar districts to discover that. They know that he is willing to work for whatever he can get, and that he will do, faithful service without attempting to change his lot through the service of labor unions—until he is absolutely in control and then you cannot say exactly what he will do for out west he has shown himself capable of nasty conduct. Hence when a reference is made to the Pole, there is apt to be a pitying smile, a shrug, or a little curl of the lip. But he has friends and they say when he is immersed in a big city he reforms his ways in a measure, even that he may one day become entirely civilized and wash as often as anybody.

The expose continued describing the terrible living conditions of the Polish sugar factory workers, describing their tenement homes as "a wretched Barrack" and the stench of their dwellings and the odor from their food. However, an 1885 government sanitary inspection of Brooklyn contradicted this disparaging image noting that a Polish colony existed on Oakland Avenue, near Box Street. Instead of the filth that the writer expected, the Polish houses and the private apartments were very clean and bright. The floors were scrubbed carefully and all the kitchen utensils shone with much polishing. Flowers blossomed in the windows and the women and children were clean, well dressed and refined looking. Each family had three rooms, one of which was large with windows. The other two were used as sleeping rooms. They had no windows. Most of the families had boarders who slept on the floor at night.

Initially disunited and used as nonunion strikebreakers, the Poles realized they were being exploited and quickly organized to demand better pay and conditions. Polish workers abandoned the sugar mills along with other workers in the unsuccessful Great Sugar Strike of 1886. In 1910, a large Polish general strike hit not only the sugar plant, but also the huge American Hemp Rope Manufacturing Company and the Chelsea Manufacturing Company, another local rope factory. Originally started as an ancillary industry for shipbuilding, the American Manufacturing Company became the largest rope maker in the world and the fourth largest employer in Brooklyn with a huge, mostly female, staff. In 1910, the plant's workers tried to occupy the factory and break through a lockout. The police clashed with Polish and Lithuanian female staff there, who pelted them with bricks, rocks and bottles. The police had to arrest several women before the riot was quelled. The strike underscored the huge role Poles played in local industry before World War I.

Polish immigration became a defining feature of Pete's Greenpoint ward thanks to the establishment of a Polish Catholic church. In 1894 Fr. Leon Wysiecki secretly purchased 10 lots on which St. Stanislaus Kostka Church now stands at the corner of Driggs Avenue and Humboldt Street. A fluent German speaker, Wysiecki had to hide his intention of building a Polish church. One of the signs of the growth of the Polish community was the opening of a second church in 1916, SS. Cyril & Methodius Parish on DuPont Street.

McGuinness was probably less than honest in his comments about his role in the Native Borns. Irish-American R.J. Hurley founded the Native Borns in 1914 as "The Sons of the State of New York." The *Eagle* asked him to weigh in on the controversy surrounding the Native Borns. He stated, "I opened the Greenpoint Council. We have several Polish members now." Members promised not to hire foreign workers, patronize foreign owned shops or vote for foreign candidates in elections. One of the Native-born members, Captain D. F. Ward, expanded on the goals of the organization, stating:

> It is our sacred duty to stand by each other and battle to the last ditch for the supremacy of the Native-Borns in the land of the Free." He continued, "We are naturally opposed to the foreign element coming here, which may be classed as the dross of Europe—the criminal, the pauper, the insane and the malcontent. We are opposed to the political bosses or home traitors who in order to gather strength at the polls make deals with foreign organizations that rob the native-born American of his vested rights and seriously interfere with the proper protection of our rights and property."

No one is quite sure how many Native-Born members Greenpoint had. One figure quoted eleven hundred and fifty active members. In 1915, McGuinness was introduced to a group of two thousand people at a Native Born picnic. World War I in large part killed the xenophobia of the "Native Borns" because the Poles fought heroically for their new country, erasing any doubts about their loyalty to America. The nativist effort failed and quickly both McGuinness and McQuade, realizing the power of the Polish vote, started printing campaign literature and ballot guides in Polish. The Poles, though, would feel unappreciated by McGuinness and left out of local political spoils. The Poles eventually gave McGuinness one of his few political defeats when in 1936, Polish-American John Smolensky defeated McGuinness' candidate and was elected to the State Assembly, becoming Greenpoint's first Polish elected official.

Chapter Sixteen: The Greenpoint Patriotic League

Without World War I Pete McGuinness never would have risen to power. He skillfully used the patriotism the war aroused to demonstrate his leadership skills and the patriotic organization that he formed during the war helped elect him to grasp political power. In 1917, when the United States entered the war, the xenophobic "Native Borns" were transformed into "The Greenpoint Patriotic League" under McGuinness' leadership. McGuinness, though not yet thirty years old, astutely presented himself as Greenpoint's most ardent patriot. His childhood friend, John MacCrate, ran the local draft board and gave Pete the names of local boys who were to be sent away. McGuinness then sat down with the draftee and the soldier's family to calm their apprehensions.

In that war, local draftees marched off together for basic training. Whenever a batch of Greenpoint boys left, they received a send-off by McGuinness and his partisans, carrying the banners of McGuinness' organizations, along with music by the Full Military Brass Band of Professor William J. Connolly, a musician, who was one of McGuinness's most important political allies. McGuinness would borrow a white horse from Orr's and ride regally at the head of the farewell parade. Pete said of his farewell parades, "Lets send 'em off with a smile," and he certainly did.

He also used the Patriotic League to attack the local political machine headed by James McQuade. McGuinness claimed that Democratic Party's district leader, James McQuade, was doing little to boost the morale of Greenpoint's soldiers. He ordered his followers to canvass the neighborhood for money to buy presents for the men going off to war. Naturally, this was a popular cause and merchants and other Greenpointers gave generously. McGuinness presented each draftee with a bon voyage package containing food, cigarettes, soap, razor blades and an inspirational leaflet by McGuinness himself. The Patriotic League even continued sending soldiers packages in France and many grateful soldiers wrote letters home thanking the Patriotic League, casting McGuinness' work in a positive light. One local boy who claimed to be the first soldier from Greenpoint to reach German soil wrote home a letter that was prominently displayed in

The Weekly Star:

> I was thinking of Greenpoint through every minute of it.
> ... In the last few months I've seen a lot of Greenpoint boys over here.
> ... I find that most of the boys feel about the way I do. They think that Peter J. McGuinness is doing very good work for Greenpoint. We sure hope he keeps it up and that Greenpoint appreciates him.

The war unified the community, healing the tension that the Native Borns had caused with the Polish community. The Poles saw World War I as a war to liberate their homeland, and hundreds of local Polish men volunteered and fought bravely. After the war, Polish veterans organizations became very important and served as a springboard for World War I veteran, State Assemblyman Smolensky's political career.

Many a morning the citizens of Greenpoint were awakened by the brass notes from Connolly's band and the sound of marching feet as the local inductees paraded off to war. The parade route led down Manhattan Avenue, then over the bridge to the train station in Long Island City. Hundreds of flag-waving citizens would come out to enjoy the spectacle, and McGuinness gained greatly in stature.

McGuinness served his country in another capacity, becoming the first lumber inspector hired by the United States government during the war. The government built wooden airplanes in World War I, and bad wood could kill an aviator. Pete's experience at Orr's gave him the expertise to evaluate shipments of lumber that went into by-planes. He traveled the entire East Coast, from Maine to Florida, inspecting practically all the lumber used by the government in the East.

Once, a group of lumberjacks mistakenly imagined that Pete with his Brooklyn accent was a New York sissy, and they started a decidedly one-sided altercation. Pete recalled, "I just took out me hammer, tapped one of the mugs on the conk and after that I was the boss."

Another time, an Army officer wanted Pete to approve a batch of substandard birch wood, but McGuinness refused, much to the officer's irritation. McGuinness inquired how much experience the officer had with birch and when the major replied none, McGuinness answered, "I have been a lumber handler all my life and I am not going to approve this batch because if some Greenpoint boy is in a plane that crashes because of bad wood, I don't want him dying with the words 'that damned McGuinness' on his lips."

McGuinness' work also brought him south for the first time when he spent time in Savannah, Georgia, whose racism and segregation shocked him. He hated the South in part because his maternal grandfather had been killed by Southerners in the Civil War. "I don't like that Jim Crow they got," he said, "and I don't like their goddam white crow no better."

After the war, Pete transformed his organization into a veteran's club to help local boys re-enter the job market and hired many veterans at Orr's lumberyard. These men and their families felt sincerely grateful to Pete, becoming some of his staunchest supporters. A hundred and twenty-eight local soldiers died in the war including the McVeigh brothers from Hausman Street, who died on the same day. The huge loss of local lives demanded a fitting monument, and McGuinness led the efforts to build one. He wanted to honor them with a statue of great beauty, so he helped fundraise for the striking bronze winged victory figure in McGolrick Park, which was created by Carl Augustus Heber (1875–1956) and dates to 1923. The statue depicts a female allegorical figure, holding aloft a modified laurel, the symbol of victory, and in her right hand supporting a large palm frond, symbol of peace. The granite pedestal is inscribed with the names of where local soldiers fought in France.

World War I had a profound effect on Greenpoint. Many men returned home grateful to McGuinness and his organization, ready to elect him to political office. The ex-soldiers founded many local veterans clubs, which became powerful new voices in local politics. These veterans' clubs became a bulwark of McGuinness' support, yet one club would also be the scene of a scandal that would not only embarrass McGuinness, but also raise questions about his ties with organized crime.

Chapter Seventeen: Political Stirrings

After the war, McGuinness emerged as a popular and widely respected community leader. He had proven to be a man of action who could mobilize ordinary Greenpointers to work together for change, yet at war's end when McGuinness looked at Greenpoint he saw not dynamism, but stagnation and even decline. Greenpoint was an area in despair and many locals who could afford it were leaving.

Property values were falling and both the city and private investors were reluctant to invest in an area, seemingly in such precipitous decline. There were a number of festering problems driving down property values and first amongst them was the industrial stink. The area was heavily polluted, and no politician was leading the fight against the factories fouling local air and water. A large group of unassimilated recent immigrants had arrived, causing overcrowding and sparking resentment at their inability to speak English and willingness to work for starvation wages. Margaret Conlon, a local poet and later political ally of McGuinness, caught the grim mood of despair in a poem published in the *Greenpoint Star*:

> Daily neighbors move to other sections
> Where buildings rise in process of erection
> Where bridges close and cars are ever moving
> Where roads and all conditions are improving.
>
> Yet, dear Greenpoint, noble town of fame
> Year after year e'er remains the same
> Through lack of unity to make a stand
> To fight for the improvements we demand.
>
> Oh, those on high who watch mere mortals act
> Send us a fighter strong, clean, and intact,
> That we may save our fair town from decay
> And from the chains of unrest break away

McGuinness decided Greenpoint needed political change and took the daring step of supporting his childhood friend, the lawyer John MacCrate, to represent Greenpoint in Congress, even though supporting MacCrate, a Republican, was a huge violation of the idea of

Democratic regularity McGuinness had always preached. McGuinness believed his friend had far more integrity than his fellow Democrats who he knew would serve the interests of the political machine first, and the area's second.

McGuinness again transformed his club, "The Greenpoint Patriotic League" into the "MacCrate Campaign Committee," but Pete realized that for a Republican to win in a district where registration of Democrats to Republicans was nine to one, the campaign needed to indict the entire local political machine and it needed to attack it in ways that had never been used before. McGuinness proved to be a master of political insurgency, running a campaign that was nothing short of revolutionary.

In 1918, traditional political campaigning was still largely conducted along personal lines and few politicians were savvy enough to use the media. Politicians mostly did events and glad-handed on street corners. McGuinness realized that for his friend to win, he had to conduct a radically new campaign through the local newspapers, but writing letters and articles seemed like a daunting task for a man without a high school education. McGuinness understood that he needed the help of someone who was literate enough to attack the establishment's inactivity in the press. He turned to the poet, Mrs.

Conlon, who became his pen. Thanks to her, McGuinness was able to place a series of letters critical of the inaction of local politicians into the local newspapers. After McGuinness' election as alderman in 1919 she served for many years as Democratic co-leader. Her ability to write made her indispensible to McGuinness.

McGuinness made the 1918 congressional elections not only an attack on the inactive local congressman, but also on the entire political machine of the District Leader James McQuade, who had recently wrested party control away from longtime leader John Carpenter. He made District Leader McQuade and his inertia the chief issue in the election, even though McQuade was not on the ballot. Every time he learned of a new grievance in the community, Conlon helped him write a letter singling out McQuade and the Tammany machine for blame. These letters often contained dubious, but damaging claims that hurt McQuade. McGuinness also charged that the sitting congressman was absent for a huge number of votes on the floor of the House, tarring him with the name, "Vanishing Joseph Flynn."

McGuiness in his letters took the guise of a long-suffering local who had grown fed up with the indifference and inaction of the local politicians. He held McQuade responsible for Greenpoint's lack of playgrounds and schools, for the deplorable condition of its roads, for the smog and foul smells from the factories, for the garbage in Newtown Creek, for gypsy encampments, and for the fact that livestock were herded through the streets of Greenpoint to abattoirs like the one on Greenpoint Avenue. Referring to the livestock, he wrote. "These animals knock over baby carriages with babies in them, and they knock down Greenpoint mothers, and the bulls kick them and knock them down, running into store windows and kicking them and breaking them. Why does Greenpoint have to put up with this? What's our dude leader Jim McQuade and his alderman and his assemblyman doing to stop these beasts?" These charges were largely fabricated, but they stuck.

After World War I, few working-class Greenpointers had indoor-plumbing, requiring them to bathe in public baths, but Greenpoint seemed to lag behind other areas in getting its fair share of public baths, and McGuinness capitalized on this. Other neighborhoods, he complained, were getting public baths and showers, but Greenpoint, which was short on domestic plumbing, was not. "What's the matter with Park Avenue Jim McQuade?" he demanded to know. "Don't he think his own people are good enough to have baths and showers? What we need around here is fighting leaders. Why shouldn't Greenpoint be right up there with Flatbush and places like that?"

McGuinness not only campaigned through the papers, but also on street corners. He proved to be a highly effective orator, and people were intrigued by the idea of a Registered Democrat stumping for a Republican. The machine found no orator who could compete with his booming voice and caustic wit.

McGuinness did not just attack the district leader. He also brazenly attacked John McCooey, the Democratic Party boss of Kings County, a formidable presence in Brooklyn at that time, who supported McQuade. McGuinness pretended to be scornful of politicians in general and presented himself merely as a person who had been driven to action by corruption, abuse, sloth and official insolence. "I have to laugh," he wrote to the editor of *The Weekly Star*, "when I think of these big bluffs of politicians coming into this district around election time, getting on the platform and telling the people what they will give them, and when elected you will never see the old blowhards again. If you ask me, all this is Mr. McCooey's work. Now, I say, let Mr. McCooey and his officeholders refuse us these improvements, and we'll show them what Greenpoint can do. Who is this McCooey, anyway? Does anyone ever see him around Greenpoint? Our motto here should be Greenpointers work for Greenpoint."

McGuinness urged MacCrate to enter the Democratic Primary and he reluctantly agreed. The chances of a registered Republican winning in a Democratic primary seemed remote, but Pete stumped hard for his childhood friend, convincing many local Democrats to take the drastic step of voting Republican to shake up the complacent establishment. Years later, McGuinness recalled a humorous incident from MacCrate's campaign. McGuinness' son George caught a boy destroying MacCarate campaign signs. The sixteen-year-old three-hundred-pound younger McGuinness confronted the boy and an altercation ensued with McGuinness wrestling him to the ground and sitting on him until the cops arrived. When Mrs. McGuinness worriedly inquired about her son, he said, "Its ok Ma, he can't lift me."

MacCarate's opponent had the backing of Mayor Hylan and seemed a shoe-in, but the political establishment was shocked when MaCrate won the primary. In a panic, the machine chose a popular Democrat, Michael Fogarty, to run against him in the general election, but shockingly, Fogarty also lost to the upstart Republican in a massively Democratic district. This was merely the first battle in McGuinness' long war against the political establishment.

The next year, Pete himself ran for alderman against

the handpicked candidate of McQuade, William McGarry. As in the previous campaign, Pete turned the election into a referendum on McQuade. He charged that McQuade was a toady of Mccooey, passively accepting Greenpoint's being shortchanged. The Jefferson Club backed Joseph Bolger, a club member, creating a three-way race, and barred McGuiness and his followers from the club he had belonged to since his youth. His supporters defiantly organized what he called the Open Air Democratic Club and held meetings on street corners.

McGuinness employed novel campaign tactics. Rather than creating banners or posters, McGuinness chose to give out small cards with his name and a curious cryptic message. He also ran these messages as small ads in the *Weekly Star*:

"The Man of the Hour. Who Is He? Peter J. McGuinness." "Vote for the Man Who will Bring Patronage to the District—Peter J. McGuinness." One display ad read:

GET ON THE LAUGH WAGON

Laugh.

The best tonic in the World is Happiness.

Laughter induces happiness,

And happiness is the theme of our existence.

McGuinness for Alderman

He continued to write provocative letters to the editor. Innumerable items appeared in the *Weekly Star*: "When you see Greenpoint's fighting candidate for Alderman, He's got some answer" and "Jim McQuade had better watch out. Peter McGuinness was down at the Du Tel Pleasure Club the other night, and the boys say the Stormy Petrel of the North End is really on the war path."

McGuinness won the three-way race by under five hundred votes. The political establishment was dumbfounded. In the general election he decimated his Republican rival by more than two thousand votes. A revolution had occurred in local politics, and soon McGuinness would become the most colorful Alderman in the history of New York City politics, shocking and delighting not only Greenpoint, but also the entire city.

Chapter Eighteen: The Most Colorful Alderman Ever

Although he was alderman-elect, McGuinness continued to work at Orr's Lumber Yard until a few hours before he was sworn in. If his election was a shock, his actions on the Board of Aldermen would prove even more outrageous. McGuinness was perhaps the most unique personality in City Hall history. His years in the lumberyard would serve him well on the board of aldermen because boisterous and rude Tammany Hall politicians dominated the Board of Aldermen in the first years that McGuinness served. Personal conflicts often marred the Board's proceedings. Insults were hurled and even fistfights occasionally broke out in the chamber.

In theory, the Board of Aldermen was the municipal equivalent of a corporate board of directors, setting public policy in relation to money, planning, zoning and public improvements. Theoretically, it controlled the budget, giving it huge power. In actuality, though, the Board of

Aldermen was limited in its power. It had to share power with the mayor, borough presidents and board of estimate, further diluting its influence. McGuinness, a man of action, was entering a body known for its passivity. Most of the aldermen were little more than functionaries. Powerful district leaders whom they were beholden to put them into office and most aldermen did nothing without the approval of these district leaders. At its worst, the board was little better than a rubber stamp for the mayor's actions.

The Tammany men looked down on the uneducated Greenpoint upstart and his Brooklynese speech, so McGuinness, an independent Democrat with little love for Tammany Hall, rebelled against their domination of the Council. McGuinness immediately caused controversy, and verbal bombast would be his trademark for all his years in the lawmaking body. He did not remain quiet for five minutes on his first day as Alderman, asking to be recognized by the President of the Board of Alderman, Fiorello La Guardia, "The Little Flower," who would become a colorful Mayor of New York City and a lifelong McGuinness friend. Greenpoint's alderman said, "Mr. Chairman, Mr. Chairman, I demand a point of order." La Guardia asked the speaker to identify himself and McGuinness in a booming voice proclaimed, "I am Peter J McGuinness and I represent the Fifteenth Assembly District, Greenpoint, the Garden Spot of the world." A Tammany alderman rudely told him to shut up and sit down. McGuinness glowered at the smaller representative and replied that he would not sit down and there was no one present who could make him sit down. Thus began the career of what many people deem to be the most colorful alderman ever in New York City history.

Once, in frustration, Ruth Pratt, who represented the Upper East Side, accused the aldermen of being mere rubber stamps for Tammany Hall and the District Leaders. McGuinness, offended, got the floor and angrily replied, "I never was, and never will be, a rubber stamp for anybody." McGuinness also expressed his frustration with the timidity of some of the aldermen saying, "You fellows should not be pictures on the wall. You come here as legislators. You have the right to criticize any commissioner. If you do not think you have that right shut up forever, go home and send up some of your old campaign posters."

McGuinness could even be menacing. When a Republican gubernatorial candidate claimed that the Democratic aldermen had blocked an investigation into the price of milk, Pete thundered that the accusation was a damned lie and continued to fulminate against the assertion, even after being ruled out of order.

McGuinness had a silver tongue and loved to work it. Arguably the most voluble representative in New York

City history, McGuinness made hundreds of speeches. He missed only two meetings during his thirteen years on the Board of Aldermen and made a long speech at almost every one he attended. "There's nothing I liked like giving a hot spiel," he once said. Later in life he reflected, "I guess me pals are glad I don't do that any more. I was getting to be a real gasbag." Years of windjammer oratory had a curious effect on him, not unlike the effect of too many blows to the head on an old boxer. He was speech-drunk. Just as an old fighter would come out swinging at the sound of a dinner bell, so McGuinness would break into a long speech at the mere mention of George Washington, Pope Pius XII, Franklin D. Roosevelt, or any other politically hallowed name.

His audiences were not always appreciative of his long-winded speeches. Once after a speech, one of the Tammany Alderman Thomas "Tin Box" Farley tripped McGuinness as he was returning to his seat. McGuinnness got up and left the room, but on his return he knocked Farley to the floor, much to the delight of the non-Tammany legislators. Years later, on a hot and humid Friday afternoon, when the other aldermen wished to adjourn for some cold brews, McGuinness announced his intention to make a statement for the record. Such statements could last over an hour and an audible groan probably filled the room. McGuinness repaired to the washroom, as was his habit to wash out his mouth. Three other aldermen followed him into the bathroom with a diabolical plan. While one of the alderman distracted McGuinness, the others stole his false teeth, preventing McGuinness from speaking, much to the delight of the assembled lawmakers.

McGuinness' joie-de-vivre and exuberance stood out amongst the often-morose functionaries. Almost always in high spirits, McGuinness sometimes found it impossible to contain his exuberance. On such occasions, he began by bouncing up and down in his chair; then he whistled a few bars of jolly music, flicked some imaginary dust from the shoulders of his coat with his fingertips, and rises to do a few jig steps. "Jeez, I am feeling spiffy today," he said when this mood was upon him and also said, "Don't mind me, pals. It's just me nature to whistle." Once he whistled and jigged in the midst of a solemn speech by a fellow alderman and was asked if the interruption was a protest of any sort. "Bejesus, no," he said. "You know me, pal the soul of music. I even got a band on me hat."

McGuinness proved himself to be an able legislator, despite his lack of formal education. However, there was one embarrassing incident that the alderman laughed about for years. There was a proposal to buy eight Venetian gondolas to place in Central Park Lake. When McGuinness heard the size of the expenditure, he thought it excessive and he rose for recognition, which LaGuardia granted. McGuinness said, "That seems like a lot of taxpayer money to spend on gondolas. Why don't we just buy a male gondola and a female gondola and let nature take its course?"

McGuinness liked many of the other aldermen, even if he disagreed with them politically. He once said, "In politics I have some enemies, but in private life I have none." When Fiorello LaGuardia defeated the Democratic candidate for mayor McGuinness graciously stated, "The Little Flower is a most splendid gentleman. Under him, we know the poor people of this city will be looked after, irregardless of what may befall. What he done, he done honest and he done good." B. Charney Vladeck, a Socialist alderman from the Lower East Side and a man who generally classed Democratic officeholders with sweatshop proprietors and exploiters of child labor, was one of his warmest admirers. "That Irisher!" Vladeck used to say: "Sometimes he makes me wish I was a Democrat."

McGuinness won Vladeck's friendship by giving Democratic sponsorship to a number of Socialist resolutions. "Many's the time," he said "I used to say, Cheeny, old pal, if you got something you really want to get through this here board, give it to me, and I'll make it Irish for you. I figured what the hell, if something was good enough for Cheeny, it was good enough for the other aldermen.

Cheeny give me a lot of contracts to put through, and all the Democrats thought they were mine and voted for them." He also befriended Republican Newbold Morris, a blue-blooded aristocrat from Yale, who was the city's ranking Republican and by far its most ardent evangel of the municipal reform McGuinness opposed, yet he found McGuinness irresistible and frequently had him to the Yale Club, despite Peter's lack of upper-class, pedigree. McGuinness wrote him the following note:

> Hon. Newbold Morris, President
> Office of the President of the Council
> City Hall, New York
>
> Dear Pal Newbold,
>
> I am in receipt of your splendid letter, and feeling as I do it was most welcome. I was just speaking of you to Judge MacCrate and Judge Lockwood, and we were discussing what a fine fellow you are.
>
> I consider you my very dearest pal, and the way you accept some of my friends who have had occasion to request favors and have been advised by them of the wonderful reception they get from you.

> Newbold, old pal, no words can express my proper feelings and thoughts about you, and while the sun is shining on the Great Irish, the sun will shine on us two, while we are enjoying that splendid luncheon at the Yale Club and basking in our wonderful friendship.
>
> Your pal,
> Pete

Perhaps the greatest indication of his refusal to let political differences prevent cross-party friendships was with Alderwoman Ruth Platt, a Republican who often voted against bills McGuinness backed. For instance, hers was the lone vote against McGuinness' proposal for the city to lend money to the newly independent Irish Free State. McGuinness' most admired speech before the Board of Aldermen was delivered upon the occasion of Pratt's resignation from the Board following her election to Congress. He delivered a warm testimonial on behalf of his fellow aldermen, which ended:

> Ruth, all we have to say is that when you go down to Washington you want to take along that beautiful fur coat that your dear husband gave you. You

> want to take that coat to Washington, Ruth, because it's very, very cold down there. Washington may be further South than New York City, but the people there are cold as ice. They don't love one another the way people here do. Why you know yourself, Ruth, that here in the Board of Aldermen of the City of New York there isn't a single man who if you were cold and unhappy couldn't put his arms around you and hug you and make you feel good. But you'll never in your life find such loving hearts in Washington. I know, Ruthie darling, because I been there and in the coldness down there I nearly froze meself to death. So you'll sure need that coat, Ruthie me darling.

Over the years McGuinness became one of the most loved aldermen on the Board. To reciprocate the affection that other men in public life had shown for him, McGuinness honored them by electing them to his Grand Benevolent Order of Pork Chops, a fraternal organization of large, but uncounted, membership. Whenever he met a member, he said, "Hello there, me old pork chop!" "It's just a kind of a humorous thing I thought up," he said reluctantly, when pressed for an explanation. He added, "What the hell, I had to have some thing to call me best pals. I call them pork chops because all the old aldermen loved eating pork chops."

The Grand Benevolent Order of Pork Chops held only one formal meeting in 1931, upon the occasion of McGuinness's retirement from the Board of Aldermen. The Board adjourned its regular meeting, and after several non-members had been admitted to the chamber, reconvened as the Pork Chops. There were many testimonials to McGuinness, and he was presented with a gold watch, a chain, and a charm that he described as "a gold statue of a pork chop." The Grand Master of the G.B.O.P.C. was Alderman Isidor Frank, a Jewish butcher who gave Democratic district leaders generous discounts on the turkeys and chickens they distributed to the poor at Thanksgiving and Christmas.

Perhaps the press never loved another city legislator as much as McGuinness. He gave any reporter an interview at any time on any subject and needed no press agent. McGuinness' outlandish statements made great copy, and if a reporter had a deadline and attributed something funny to the alderman that McGuinness had not said, he would never contradict the reporter. The normally staid *New York Times* and other papers humorously referred to him at various times as " the Czar of Greenpoint," "the Napoleon of Greenpoint," " the Laird of Greenpoint," "the Metternich of Greenpoint," "the Taoiseach of Greenpoint"," "the boss of Greenpoint" and of course "the king of the Garden Spot."

During the twenties, he was the subject of a blizzard of stories. A comment by McGuinness on Prohibition, the New Woman, or the war debts, frequently accompanied by a picture of the Alderman striking an aggressive pose alongside MacMonnies' statue of Civic Virtue in City Hall Park, was almost a regular feature in the afternoon papers.

The New York Times wrote a tongue-in-cheek report about McGuinness' pitching in the annual baseball game between the Aldermen and the city reporters. The headline read:

> **McGuinness Upset by Baseball Plot**
>
> **Pride of Greenpoint Unable to Throw a Strike**

Mayor LaGuardia, the game's umpire, took part in a reporters' plot to play a practical joke on McGuinness who was the alderman's starting pitcher. LaGuardia agreed never to call any of McGuinness' pitches strikes. The *Times* gleefully reported:

> In the hot sun the delegate from Greenpoint gave it his best, but before doubt darkened his innocence the bases were full and the reporters heart-

> ened. His brow knitted and his fists clenched, he called to the umpire, "Hey, it stands to reason that a man must throw a strike sometime in his life." The mayor nodded, but the game was young yet. The McGuinness shook his head dubiously and turned to the batter. He had been up against raw deals before. His patience had been proof against all of them and justice had triumphed. But after eleven runs had been scored with the end of the first inning nowhere in sight and aldermanic demands for his retirement becoming louder, The McGuinness' patience was taxed. One final pitch and then "Ball, called the mayor in a monotonous voice. "Right over here" the Greenpoint star insisted, indicating a waist high pitch. "Way up here" the umpire declared diffidently hand high over his head. In desperation, McGuinness flung the ball over the backstop and stormed off the field. "Strike" called the mayor. At that the Greenpoint star realized the situation. It was what he had always read about: secret conspiracies, backhanded plots, dark plots pulled right under his nose.

McGuinness gave reporters his best copy, though, in staunch defense of New York. When a Congressman Gossett from Texas doubted if New Yorkers were real

Americans, McGuinness replied, "If this guy Gossett, or whatever his name is, is the kind of people they have in Texas, then they ought to give it back to Mexico." He liked to give out statements defending New Yorkers against bluenose attacks on their city. His favorite adversary was the Board of Temperance, Prohibition, and Public Morals of the Methodist Episcopal Church. McGuinness answered its every charge. When it accused New Yorkers of general immorality, he replied, "New York is the cleanest city on earth. You can't find a more moral race of people anywhere." When New York's theaters were under attack, he said, "The theaters of New York are great educational institutions. Some people would be happy if Broadway was a pasture. The hell with them! I'm for the Great White Way." When New York language was said to be profane and obscene, McGuinness was irate. "There's no more profanity here than in Peapatch," he stated, and added, "New Yorkers may swear a lot on their impulses, but they never swear from the heart." To the complaint that New York women exposed too much of themselves, McGuinness replied, "New York has the healthiest air in the country. What if the girls do go in for few clothes? The good air gets to their bodies and makes them healthier. Look at Adam and Eve. They weren't all bundled up. Think how many descendants they had. Good night, there's no harm in women wearing few clothes."

McGuinness left the Board of Aldermen after twelve years for a better paying federal position, but many rued his decision. Summarizing his service in 1931, the year he resigned, he said that he had driven the cows and pigs from the streets of Greenpoint and chased three hundred Chinese out of the district. ("You can't make a vote out of a million of 'em, "he said) In his farewell speech he listed his achievements while on the Board, "I drove nine gypsy bands out of Greenpoint as well as cats and dogs that used to run down the streets. One of the best things I done was to establish a farm garden so that children could learn the value of real vegetables. I got Greenpoint three playgrounds, the subway, a million-and-a-half dollar bridge and two million dollars in paving. I done good. I thank you."

Some of his friends and admirers felt that he made a large mistake in deserting the board of aldermen for the obscurity of a county office. A writer in the *Brooklyn Eagle* compared his departure from City Hall with the "Caesar's departing Rome for Constantinople or the Pope's retirement to Avignon." He admitted in later life that no other job was ever so much fun as his stint as alderman, and he left a huge void at City Hall. After his departure New York lawmaking would never again be so much fun.

Chapter Nineteen: Fighting Social Change

McGuinness served as alderman during a time of huge social and cultural change. The alderman was an outspoken opponent of two of the most prominent social changes that took place after the war: the emancipation of women and the prohibition of alcohol, ushered in by the 18th amendment

McGuinness began his first term at the end of World War I when female behavior was rapidly changing. Female flappers defied traditional ladylike behavioral expectations by cutting their hair short, wearing pants, instead of skirts, and, most shocking for McGuinness, even smoking in public. These rule-breaking new women, like Greenpoint's Mae West, flouted conventions, shocking traditionalists like McGuinness. Smoking was not just considered unladylike; it was for many a black mark on a woman's character. A *Washington Post* editorial in 1914 declared, "A man may take out a woman who smokes for a good time, but he won't marry her, and if he does, he won't stay married."

In 1921, he proposed an ordinance in the Board of Aldermen banning women from smoking in public places. The bill was misfiled as a law, although it was never enforced. McGuinness, asked to explain proposing the law, answered, "Young fellows go into our restaurants to find women folks sucking cigarettes. What happens? The young fellows lose all respect for the women, and the next thing you know the young fellows, vampired by these smoking women, desert their homes, their wives and children, rob their employers and even commit murder so that they can get money to lavish on these smoking women."

McGuinness later realized that he had gone too far and tried to backtrack from his earlier position. "Everybody got me wrong," McGuinness reportedly told his colleagues. "I didn't introduce the resolution as a blue law. I did not intend to stop the ladies from smoking in public places. My idea was to make the proprietors of these places fix up nice smoking rooms for the ladies to enjoy their little smoke."

McGuinness' exculpatory comments did not impress fellow alderman Bruce M. Falconer, who charged that McGuinness was guilty of "deliberate cowardice against the ladies," to which McGuinness replied shouting, "There never was a drop of cowardice in my blood. I come from a people with real blood, who would die for anything they would do; that's me!"

Ironically, McGuinness was a champion for repealing prohibition, even though he himself was a teetotaler. This "wet" position made good political sense in Greenpoint, an area notorious for speakeasies and illicit stills. One estimate said that there were eight hundred speakeasies in his district, but when McGuinness was asked if this figure was accurate, he replied that he had no knowledge of any speakeasies in Greenpoint.

McGuinness wisely understood the lunacy of trying to enforce such an unpopular law in an area where the vast majority of people were drinkers. Greenpoint was a hotbed of bootlegging and thousands of people broke the law, causing a backload of cases for the overwhelmed court system. A typical prohibition case involved local judge: Magistrate Thomas Dale vented his wrath on poor Thomas Solohoski, twenty years of age, of Engert Street, arrested for public intoxication. Judge Dale asked Solohoski where he had had gotten that poisonous rum, but even if he knew, Solohoski wasn't telling. He told the judge he did not remember where he had been drinking. The judge could no longer contain his frustration and told Solohoski, "Of course, you can't remember. How could you when you drink that stuff they are selling?" The judge continued, "There are more speakeasies in the Eastern District, I feel, than any other place in the borough. You can get a drink in candy shops, in cigar stores, hat stores, bootblack parlors, hardware stores and finely appointed apartments. It wouldn't take me long to get a line on them and if I got busy I would close up every one of these places and put those selling this poison in jail." The angry magistrate thundered, "If I had the time and could get together twenty-five red blooded men I would clean up the speakeasies in Greenpoint in twenty-four hours."

One of McGuinness' major objections to prohibition was the intrusive enforcement government used to enforce the law. The states and the federal Government were intended to enforce the law concurrently, so New York State passed the Mullen-Gage Act to enforce the provisions of Prohibition, which allowed the police to enter a home suspected of producing or storing alcohol without a warrant—a clear violation of the Fourth Amendment. Even though the Mullen-Gage Act was repealed, the police continued warrantless home searches. In November of 1924, McGuinness angered the supporters of the Temperance movement by proposing the abolition of the Special Service Squad that conducted such home searches. McGuinness argued that the cops who enforced anti-alcohol laws should be reassigned to stop street crime—a much greater social menace. He stated, "The prohibition question is a national one, not local. Put the members of the Special Service Squadron on the streets where they belong, instead of having them snoop in and about dives that sell whiskey and beer."

McGuinness' proposal drew the ire of Police Commissioner Enright, who called him, "a two-cent politician who represents a district near Newtown Creek." McGuinness replied, "I deem it an honor to be placed in the same class as Washington, Lincoln, Harding and Grant, all of whom had their picture on the two- cent stamp." New York contributed no more valiant or resourceful battler than McGuinness to the war against the Eighteenth Amendment. He probably made more attempts to find a legal way around Prohibition than any other legislator in the country. "America does not want to be a dry country," he told his fellow aldermen.

"New York will never be arid. Let us keep the parched desert in the torrid countries and permit New York and her sister states to be peopled by real humans." No epidemic of grippe or head colds could strike the city without McGuinness putting before the board a resolution petitioning Congress to "so amend the Prohibition Law as to allow the sale of spirit liquors for the benefit of the sick." "It's a criminal shame," McGuinness, said, "to allow whiskey to lie idle while people are lying at death's door who could be saved by it."

McGuinness even led hundreds of indignant anti-Prohibition Greenpoint protestors in a Manhattan march behind Connolly's Marching Band called "Jimmy Walker's Beer Parade." He worked Greenpoint up to such a fury that in 1933, when the vote for repeal of Prohibition was held, Greenpoint voted eighty to one for repeal, the solidest vote, he said, and probably correctly, in the country.

McGuinness gained a lot of support for his anti-Prohibition stance, but turning a blind eye to bootleggers later had damaging political consequences for McGuinness. An incident at one of his veterans' clubs would lead to damaging allegations against McGuinness and questions about his honesty.

Chapter Twenty: The Feud

Feuds often define a time and place: Verona had the Montagues and the Capulets; West Virginia had the Hatfields and the McCoys. Greenpoint had the McGuinnesses and the McQuades. The feud lasted fifteen years, dominating local politics and richly entertaining the gossiping tongues of Greenpointers. An *Eagle* reporter once quipped, "Greenpoint was not so much a garden spot as a battleground. "Some of the liveliest primary fights in local Democratic history occurred there, but the quip was written before the height of the McGuinness-McQuade feud.

There was a rich irony to the feud because McGuinness and James McQuade were in many ways similar. They were both born on the Eagle Street, both from very large Irish-American families, both witty, both claiming to be regular Democrats, both politicians and both very competitive. The fact that the two had political clubs directly across the street from one another on the corner of Manhattan and Meserole Avenues, only added to the irony and bitterness of the feud.

In some respects, however, conflict was inevitable. Obviously, both men wanted to be leader, but there were profound differences in how they wanted to run Greenpoint. McQuade was a Tammany Hall Democrat, a loyal and obedient believer in the political machine. He got his job as registrar thanks to the insistence of Tammany Boss Charles Murphy, who forced Brooklyn Boss John McCooey to appoint him. For McQuade loyalty to the machine and its needs came first, while Greenpoint's needs came second.

McGuinness was an anti-Tammany candidate who blamed the area's ills on the corruption and neglect inherent in machine politics. For many years the Brooklyn machine tried its level best to replace him with McQuade, and over the years the dispute between the alderman and the registrar grew in intensity. The quarrel began with McGuinness' attacks on McQuade during his first campaign for alderman. McQuade took offense, vowing to crush the insurgent McGuinness.

In the next election McQuade devised an ingenious plan. He would unseat McGuinness by nominating a more educated man to run against the former lumber handler. McGuinness' leadership was briefly threatened by the appearance of a brash young attorney who argued that a forward-looking community should have as leader a person of culture and refinement, such as himself. Higher learning was enjoying immense prestige at the time, and the articulate young lawyer impressed a good many blue-collar Democratic voters with his Brooklyn Law School vocabulary. McGuinness, with his limited education, working-class speech and lack of academic vocabulary, seemed out of his depth and destined to lose the election, but he disposed of the interloper with a strategy tailor-made for his working class constituents.

The attorney challenged the alderman to a debate, which McGuinness accepted. After the challenger had finished a fancy, erudite presentation full of high-sounding phrases, McGuinness rose and glared down at the audience of shirt-sleeved laborers and housewives in aprons. Then he bellowed, "All of yez that went to Yales or Cornells raise your right hands." Not a hand went up. There was some nervous tittering in the audience. "The Yales and Cornells can vote for him," he said. "The rest of yez vote for me." They did, but McGuinness would retaliate.

In 1924, McGuinness decided to run against McQuade for Democratic Party district leader and a tough fight ensued. McQuade had the backing of McCooey's county machine and party patronage created a web of loyal families to vote for him. McQuade's own very large family was also a formidable voting block in an area where clan allegiance determined votes. McGuinness, though, had weapons at his disposal. He was an excellent stump speaker and far more charismatic than McQuade. His message of outrage over the lack of civic improvements the machine had bestowed on Greenpoint resonated with the residents. A relentless campaigner, McGuinness vowed, "I'll fight that man until he is beat. Don't forget it. He will know he is in a fight when I get started. "Asked if he enjoyed battling McQuade, he said, "What Irishman does not enjoy a good fight?" and in the 1924 campaign his tenacity won him the title of "The Fighting Alderman."

McGuinness believed less in the signs which most candidates put up in store windows than in throwaways the size of calling cards. "With them, they got something they can carry around and think about," he said. One of them read:

> VOTE FOR MCGUINNESS; MCQUADE CANNOT BE TRUSTED
>
> QUINN (FLOPPER) HAS NO PRINCIPLES
> ELIMINATE THE SOREHEADS VOTE FOR MC-GUINNESS

And another:

> DON'T MIND THE DARN FOOLS
> THEY DON'T KNOW WHAT IT'S ALL ABOUT
>
> EVEN THOUGH THEY WOULD BE NOMINATED
> THEY WOULDN'T KNOW WHAT IT IS TO BE A
> LEGISLATOR NOMINATE EXPERIENCED MEN
> VOTE MG GUINNESS AND DOYLE

And still another:

> GREENPOINT'S DICTIONARY: Wigwam Club; noun; a combination of political derelicts, cast on the island of Wigwam, with a sole purpose of doing nothing, only disrupting the democracy of Greenpoint.
>
> Object of these Derelicts: Horn-blowing, wandering from one organization to another (no end) doing nothing for the welfare of the public, and trying to get a job without taking a Civil Service Examination
>
> VOTE FOR ALDERMAN Peter J. McGuinness

Greenpoint was in political fever as the campaign raged for two months. There were non-stop meetings, myriad street corner orators and the occasional donnybrook. In the final week of the campaign McGuinness supporters held twenty outdoor rallies. McGuinness said of the April 1st primary day, "April first will be April Fool's Day for McQuade supporters." On election eve a three hundred car caravan, horns blowing, toured the district drumming up support for McGuinness, while drawing threats, curses and thrown objects from McQuade backers. McGuinness seemed to possess demonic energy as he toured the ward, making sure that his message reached every voter.

The position of the two clubs directly across Manhattan Avenue from each other added to the animosity of the campaigns. At times during the years of conflict each man's backers would open the club windows to hear the other candidate's acrimonious denunciations carrying across Manhattan Avenue. A supporter would catch some nasty phrase and then run to either the alderman or the registrar, reporting the calumny just uttered. Outraged, the alderman or the registrar would reply with some equally nasty denunciation, adding fuel to the already hot fire of the feud.

Years later, McGuinness recalled the level of conflict the two men's enmity created as night after night the rival leaders would address their followers from their clubhouse steps. The crowds spilled into the middle of Manhattan Avenue, and there were frequent border incidents. "Bejesus, I don't like to think how many busted noses there must have been," McGuinness said. "And shiners there must have been ten thousand."

On Election Day the overwrought Alderman was shocked to see an enormous amount of snow blanketing Greenpoint, and he feared that the inclement weather might dampen turnout, handing victory to his archrival. The machine got its supporters to the polls, despite the snow, and McGuiness backers were worried. In the end when the votes were counted he won a squeaker, winning 3257 to 3003, a margin of only two hundred and fifty-four votes, but McGuinness now was in a dominant political position he would hold for almost a quarter century. His hard campaigning had truly paid off.

Four years later, Brooklyn Democratic Leader John McCooey feared that the feud would so divide the Democrats that the Republicans would get elected. He worked out a compromise. McGuinness would support McQuade for registrar, and in return McQuade would recognize McGuinness as district leader and would even join his club. McQuade signed a document stating that he would join McGuinness' club; however, recognizing McGuinness' dominance was too bitter a pill for his rival to swallow and McQuade reneged on his promises to McCooey, which only increased the rancor between the two men. McQuade decided to run for district leader one more time, against the wishes of McCooey.

The feud seemed to reach its highest level of bitterness on March 21, 1928, when the *Daily Eagle* Headline proclaimed:

> **"If Pete McGuinness Meets Jim McQuade in the Street Fists May Fly Rumor Hath It."**

The article gleefully described the fisticuffs that would occur if the two met somewhere on Manhattan Avenue before the April primary:

> Other things of a sensational nature will follow. McGuinness tall, heavy of build and red-faced is likely to strike out and punch McQuade in the nose. McQuade short, stocky and red-faced is likely to strike back immediately and blood is likely to flow. All Greenpoint is agog over it, or if not, should be.

The article captured the excitement in the air in those days before the primary, noting that both clubhouses were packed to capacity and had never been fuller. Both sets of supporters scoured Greenpoint looking for votes and both clubs heard vitriolic denunciations of the other from their leader. It described with ill-concealed joy how McGuinness, "The younger and more excitable man spoke for nearly an hour and taunted his rival with having placed ten of his family in no-show jobs on the registrar payroll, paying them a total annual salary of more than $12,000 annually." McGuinness excoriated his rival, calling him "Park Avenue Jim", "Payroll Jim" and "Gentleman Jim," epithets that were insults in Greenpoint. At one point, in agitation, McGuinness said, "McQuade is the greatest liar Greenpoint has ever known." Other members of the club also attacked McQuade. Club Officer John Imperatore wrote a letter to Italian Americans of Greenpoint saying that McQuade called Italian-Americans, "guineas." All manner of villainy was ascribed to McQuade.

McGuinness supporters even penned a popular poem ridiculing McQuade and his many relatives drawing government salaries: Payroll Jim.

> They were four-by-four oh yes, fifty or more
> on the payroll of Registrar McQuade.
> There were John and Tim, Joe and Jim.
> Not a single one was afraid

They got our money like milk and honey
Every payday was a raid.
It brought tears to the eyes of rent paying guys
It was the dream of the payroll parade.

With their main and might they worked all night
On the payroll of Registrar McQuade.
Jim's family strong who worked all day long
Once a month went down to get paid
It was the dream of the payroll parade.

Then came Dr. Allen, upright and gallant.
He soon had them all afraid.
Now, they all come on time, punch the time clock
on time
in my dream of the payroll parade.

And on April third, the tread will be heard
Of the greatest of all parades.
Voters by the score, will elect McGuinness once
more
And away from Jim will the payroll fade.

McQuade and his minions were every bit as vitriolic. The *Eagle* quoted him attacking McGuinness, "This man in my humble opinion is the greatest disaster to ever hit this district." McQuade attacked his rival for his inability to bring patronage home to Greenpoint (The same attack that McGuinness had made against him years earlier) He took exception when McGuinness used the pronoun "we" in talking about Greenpoint, stating that McGuinness had no right to speak for all Greenpointers and then in a less than statesmanlike moment stated, "The J in Peter J. McGuiness stands for Jackass." McQuade explained to his followers that the alderman had called him, "a rat, a double-crosser" and "a snake-in-the grass." He said, "McGuinness in his quest for cheap publicity has been harmful to Greenpoint. Whenever Greenpoint is mentioned there is a laugh because McGuinness has made us look ridiculous to the outside world."

The registrar also took umbrage at the threat of physical violence McGuinness offered, and said, "I didn't know I had to be a Tunney (A famous contemporary boxer) to win the leadership, but if I have to in catch-as-catch-can weights I can pretty much hold my own." Other speakers followed the registrar and each offered ringing denunciations of the "jackass" alderman from across Manhattan Avenue. McQuade's ally, Assistant District Attorney Cuff, bitterly, but tactfully denounced the Alderman stating McGuinness might well be referred to as an "insect not mentioned in the best of company." He added, "If we paid any attention to the vile slanders from across the road and tried to answer them, we would be involved in a veritable flea-chase." Assistant District Attorney Cuff said, "You ought to see him on the first and the fifteenth of the month at City Hall. He is the first in line to get his check." The McQuade supporters laughed at the tiny park he acquired for the area at the end of DuPont Street, calling it a two-by-four park. They claimed that the streets were in deplorable condition and that McGuinness had been promising to get the area a high school, but had not succeeded.

McGuinness, learning of the bitter attacks leveled against him in the McQuade club, said, "Unless Park Avenue Jim McQuade quits making those false accusations against me I may find it necessary to have the Supreme Court Justice of this district appoint a lunacy commission to look into his sanity." He concluded by saying, "Next week I will try to dispel the lies that that snake in the grass across the road will cook up in the meantime."

McQuade had secured a position with the City Taxi Commission. On the eve of the election, McQuade took a page out of the McGuinness playbook when he organized a huge motorcade through Greenpoint led by over a hundred taxis. The race was too close to call in the final days. When all the votes were counted again, McGuinness prevailed by the razor slim margin of 3639 votes to 3508, just over a hundred votes separated the two rivals.

The feud only ended a few years later, when damaging revelations about McQuade ended his political career. For years, Greenpoint was notorious for the feud and even people outside Greenpoint laughed about it. Senator William Love wrote a poem about the primary conflicts in Gowanus and Greenpoint, which was a parody of the poem "Casey at the Bat." He wrote:

> We have read of Pete McGuinness and his rival James McQuade
>
> How each pursued the other and how each was unafraid.
>
> How Greenpoint and Gowanus had a corking primary scrap and how the illustrious statesman knocked the other off the map.

The feud raged on for years and it would only end after a startling revelation about McQuade put him on the front page of all the city newspapers.

Chapter Twenty-One: The Fighting Alderman from Greenpoint

Years later, McGuinness was reminiscing about the pugilists on the Board of Aldermen. He said, "All the best heavyweights were there then and I challenged them — Ed Sullivan, Mort Moses and Frank Cunningham. All of them." None dared fight him because, as he explained, "They knew they would not stand a chance."

His fights were not limited to City Hall. The alderman was once strolling through McCarren Park where he saw a gang of local thugs throw firecrackers into a baby carriage that so frightened the mother she passed out. Pete ran up to the gang and flew into action, knocking out three before they knew what hit them. He ran down the other two, knocking them out as well and then quieting the child until the mother regained consciousness.

McGuinness believed that he had to fight not only for the people of his district, but also for the people of the city. Sadly, the people meant for him Caucasians, and Mc-

Guinness was guilty of prejudice and xenophobia towards Asians and Gypsies. In 1923, McGuinness was outraged that Chinese men were cleaning city streets. He said:

> I saw the Chinamen with my own eyes and in my own district. It is a shame and it is a disgrace to the city that the Street Cleaning Commissioner should descend to the employment of those yellow men who are not American citizens when there are plenty of our own kind looking for jobs. I can't see why some of you may think it is a joke, but it is not. It is a mighty serious business to see these Chinamen who are not even citizens of the United States getting $5.15 a day each from the Street Cleaning Department when they do half the work that is demanded of a white citizen. I insist on the appointment of an investigating committee whether the Street Cleaning Commissioner has any right to employ Chinamen to do his work.

One of McGuinness' lifelong boasts was that he drove illegal Chinese out of Greenpoint. In 1922, the aldermen started to receive complaints about Chinese immigrants who crowded local boarding houses. A local box factory illegally employed a contingent of Chinese laborers who came in vans under cover of night, and housed three hundred of them inside the factory. McGuinness approached Federal officials, who did nothing to stop the Chinese from working illegally.

He confronted the factory owner personally, who said, "What of it? I save dough." Then McGuinness looked around and said, "It seems to me that you are violating a couple of ordinances. Guess I'll speak to the Building Department." The illegals were fired before nightfall.

McGuinness made *The New York Times* the next day on August 12, 1922, when a feature dramatized how he led a raid of a boarding house on Meeker Avenue that led to the arrest of seven Chinese nationals staying there. The article went on to explain that he would not rest until they were all deported. He stated, "A white man hasn't got a chance when these Chinamen are brought in to work for practically nothing." He finished saying, "I intend to see that there are none left in Greenpoint." The Chinese were found to be seamen on shore leave without the right to work legally. They were arrested and deported. McGuinness contacted Federal immigration officials, who promised to watch Greenpoint piers to prevent any more Chinese from jumping ship.

A Greenpoint poet celebrated Pete's ridding the area of the illegals in a verse published in *The Daily Star*:

When we heard that the coolies were after our

job
And our daily bread they were trying to rob
Then we needed a leader we were sure would be with us,
Then our old pal came forward, Peter McGuinness.

It was not just Chinese people who were driven out of Greenpoint. McGuinness also targeted Gypsies, whom he considered thieves. In 1928, he created a "flying column" of young boys and men that stoned a building on Oakland Street housing gypsies. He bragged about driving nine gypsy bands out of the area. "They are a menace to the garden spot of the universe. Five years ago I drove the coolies out of my district and I will keep on with the crusade until every gypsy is out of my District." He issued a victory proclamation. "I hereby declare Greenpoint to be free from Gypsies. There is nobody here now, but Democrats and some Republicans." But they kept coming back, so he said, "I will not permit any gypsy troupes to settle in my district." He added, "They frighten children, intimidate grownups, and steal at every opportunity. They are a menace to the Garden Spot of the Universe."

It was not only foreigners that McGuinness targeted, but also domestic troublemakers. In the 1920s the Ku Klux Klan was spreading its message of intolerance all over the North, including Greenpoint. The Klan began recruiting members locally under the auspices of Dr. Oscar Haywood, Klokard of the Klan in New York City. McGuinness spoke out against the Klan and declared that there was no place for the Klan in Greenpoint and that the Klan's presence in such a heavily Catholic area would cause violence. He said without any irony, "The age of bigotry has passed," and added, "When the know-nothings get control they try to say that all men are created equal except Negroes, foreigners and Catholics." Hatred, though, had not left Greenpoint. Two years later, when McGuinness campaigned for Al Smith, the first Catholic presidential nominee, he received an anti-Irish Catholic piece of hate mail that he kept until the end of his life. The hand-written note read, "Don't flatter yourself that New Yorkers like Catholics. They like them like poison. If the whole bunch of Micks would go back to Ireland where they belong New Yorkers would say good riddance to bad rubbish. "

Pete also was a relentless fighter for local infrastructure projects who realized that to win civic improvements for his area, he had to develop good relations with the mayor. He had a mutual admiration for Mayor Jimmy Walker and Walker's love for McGuinness manifested itself in many projects that improved Greenpoint. He told McGuinness, "Pete you're my favorite alderman.

You know what you want and you do not care who likes it." He continued, "Anything that Pete McGuinness wants he'll bring back to Greenpoint in the way of public improvements." One of those things McGuinness dearly wanted was a crosstown subway line, and McGuinness so charmed Walker that the mayor promised him in 1925, that construction of the line would begin in Greenpoint. Years later, in 1933, Walker wrote of the J.J. Byrne Bridge and his admiration for McGuinness:

> It would not be an exaggeration to say that I have met half a million people around the world. I cannot think of anyone whose friendship would mean more to me than that of my old pal, Peter McGuinness. The old Pal who got a bridge by the force of his personality and the promise to take his first drink when the bridge was opened.

Long after his resignation from office, Walker returned, but tarred with graft, no Democrat would befriend him, let alone employee him. McGuinness, though, never turned his back on Walker. When the ex-mayor returned in disgrace from Paris in 1942, McGuinness met him at a Brooklyn pier, threw his arms around him, and said, in the presence of the press, "Jimmy darling, me old pal, stay in Brooklyn if they won't give you a job over there. I'm sheriff here, and you can be me first deputy, me dear old pork chop."

McGuinness was a relentless advocate for his constituents' interests. An example of his ability to deliver for Greenpoint was his campaign for farm gardens for Greenpoint children. World War I produced a shortage of vegetables, so the city used the parks as gardens tended by school children. McGuinness learned that the Greenpoint children enjoyed working in the gardens, and after the war he persuaded the city administration to let them continue. After a few years, however, when his skill at legislative maneuver was getting Greenpoint far more than its fair share of appropriations for improvement, the Board of Estimate tried to clip Pete's wings, arguing that the gardens cost too much. To keep the gardens McGuinness was forced to employ his large talent for guile. One year he got his garden funds from a reluctant Board by announcing that, to show how much the children benefited from the gardens, he was going to bring six hundred of them to City Hall for a Board of Estimate meeting. "I knew that would scare the bejesus out of them," he said. He told a Board secretary that he had chartered several buses to bring them over. "They'll need a lot of room, God bless them," he said, "because I want them to have their little rakes and shovels and hoes to show how much they love tilling the soil." The prospect of six hundred youngsters thus armed produced immediate assurance from Mayor Hylan that he would vote for the appropriation.

The following year, McGuinness got the appropriation by nominating Mayor Hylan for president of the United States. He said that he argued unsuccessfully for an hour before the Board. "The sweat run down me back," he recalled. "All me nerves was jumping. I could just see them kids when I had to tell them there would be no gardens. Then it just come to me. It burst right into me brain. I made it up as I went along." He said:

> Mr. Mayor, in the history of our glorious country, there have been Two great Presidents. One was the Honorable George Washington, Who led the nation to freedom, and the other was the Honorable Abraham Lincoln, who freed the poor slaves in 1865. Ever since 1865, A pair of old black shoes have been standing beside the President's desk in the White House. Those shoes are old and worn, but they stay there in the White House because they know that the man who used to walk around in them was loved in the hearts of the poor people of America. And he loved the poor people too, Mr. Mayor. He was the man that said that God must have loved the poor people because he made so many of them. Now when they laid Abraham Lin-

> coln away, those shoes came walking back to the White House and got themselves beside his desk, and they've been waiting there ever since for a man who loves the poor people as much as he did to come and fill them. Today, Mr. Mayor, the City of New York is going to fill those shoes with one of its own, John Francis Hylan, who in his splendid wisdom in voting for these farm gardens is bringing happiness into the hearts of the little ones of Greenpoint and is showing his people, and the Great Democratic Party, which has always fought for the poor people, that he loves them too. John Francis Hylan will be the next President of the United States.

Mayor Hylan cast his three votes for the appropriations. The next morning's papers ran stories headlined "Hylan for President Move Started by Local Democratic Leader." When reporters interviewed McGuinness, he avoided most of their questions. He had a wry smile. "Hylan's a splendid man," he said, "One of the highest-type men in the country today." When he was finally pinned down, however, he said, "What the hell, pals, I don't mind giving out a few nominations if it will help Greenpoint."

One of his other major fights was for was the Greenpoint ferry. McGuinness began a tireless fight for the city to acquire the ferry, which was run by a private company. Relentlessly haunting the Board of Estimate and the City Sinking Fund, making long speech after long speech, he so wore down the mayor that Hylan grew irritated with the pesky Greenpoint alderman. Hylan asked McGuinness to the alderman's astonishment if he was in favor of city acquisition of the line. "I certainly am in favor of it," said McGuinness half in shock. The perturbed mayor shouted, "Then keep quiet and maybe you'll get what you want." McGuinness left the meeting beaming.

One of his most notable achievements was keeping a ferry running for thirteen years after it had long ago ceased paying for itself and was costing city taxpayers a lot of money. For a half-century, this ferry service to East Twenty-Third Street provided Greenpoint with its only direct communication with Manhattan and McGuinness was determined that it should be continued for the few who did commute on it. Every year he successfully appeared before the Board of Estimate to appeal for its continuance. McGuinness said that the air and sun of a ferry trip was better for newborn mothers and their children than fifty doctors. Once, addressing himself to Jimmy Walker, who as mayor presided over the board meetings and cast three of the Board's eight votes, he concluded a long speech by saying:

> Please don' t take away the old ferry, Mr. Mayor. It would be like separating an old couple that has been together for years to divorce Manhattan and Greenpoint. There would be tears of sorrow in the eyes of the old ferryboats as there would be tears in the eyes of the people of Greenpoint if them splendid old boats were put to rot in some dry dock or sold at public auction. Tell me, Mr. Mayor, now tell me, that you will love them old ferryboats in December as you did in May. (Walker was the author of a maudlin song entitled "Will You Love Me in December as You Did in May.")

"I do love them, Peter, and I love you. You're my favorite Alderman," Walker said. The ferries kept running. The next year McGuinness came up with the story that the boats were valuable relics; they had, he claimed to have learned, been used as Union troop transports on the Mississippi in the Civil War. Abraham Lincoln, he said, "would turn over in the sod" if the ferries were discontinued and destroyed. Again the ferry funds were appropriated.

Chapter Twenty-Two: Birth of the McGuinness Club

In 1924, although he had already been alderman for four years, McGuinness still had no political club of his own, posing a large political liability. Despite defeating McQuade and assuming the mantel of district leader, McGuinnness, nevertheless, had to accept McQuade's nominations for congress and for assemblyman. After defeating McQuade in the election for district leader, McGuinness was now ready to start his own club. He formed the Greenpoint People's Regular Democratic Club in part because his childhood club, the Jefferson Club, had barred him from membership. McGuinness's club would quickly dwarf the older clubs both in membership and in level of enthusiasm. A thriving political club was a sign to higher-ups in the Brooklyn Democratic Party of power and popularity. During McGuinness's lifetime the club had fifteen hundred dues paying members. Despite the large number of people who joined the club, Pete knew the names and faces of each member.

Many people joined the club because of Pete's charisma and charm. His charm even inspired people to write verse in his honor. Richard Rovere noted in 1948, "Possibly the greatest tribute to McGuinness's standing in Greenpoint is the flowering of the lyric spirit he has inspired. It may well be that more poetry has been written about him than about anyone in American politics since Abraham Lincoln." An example, from *The Weekly Star*, is an epic ballad of twenty-three verses by Maurice Dee, which begins:

> There's a man in our town whom you all know well,
> A few things about him I'm now going to tell
> He's tall, broad, and handsome, with a smile that has won us
> You can easily guess he is Peter McGuinness.

McGuinness adored every aspect of the club, spending huge amounts of time there. He loved the help he gave to his constituents, and said he could think of few pleasanter ways to spend an evening than to sit behind his bare and battered desk in the clubhouse of the Greenpoint People's Regular Democratic Organization accepting "contracts, "I get one hell of a kick out of that," he said. "Sometimes I even do favors for people in Jersey."

McGuinness realized that the secret to an effective club was keeping the members active, and there were numerous social events. The main social event of the year was the annual McGuinness Night, a black-tie affair that was held in the Labor Lyceum the first Saturday after Lent and caused a considerable upswing in the tuxedo-rental business. Another occasion of note was the Monster McGuinness Theatre Party, held in the late fall at Loew's Meserole, and still others were Ye Olde McGuinnesse Farme Barne Dance Nighte, a harvest celebration, and the McGuinness Cotton Blossom Showboat Night, a midsummer cruise on a chartered river boat.

If there was one event that McGuinness was most focused on, then it was his Christmas Eve holiday basket giveaway. The proceeds from the McGuinness Gala were used to fund the baskets. Before the Great Depression, up to eight hundred needy families received Baskets that included a turkey, coffee, tea, potatoes, cranberries, oranges, sugar and even toys for children—all items poor families could not afford. After the Depression hit, the number of charity baskets rose to two thousand, but McGuinness and his club still managed to meet the increased demand.

McGuinness might have done himself damage in the

eyes of women by proposing the smoking ban, but he understood that with female suffrage, politics was no longer a male-dominated activity and women were a vital part of the club. He stated, "Sooner or later the male members of political clubs will realize that women are in earnest about learning the who, what, where, when and why of government." He was also aware of how vital women were behind the scenes, saying, "It has been said that it is the women members that keep a political club running when a campaign is not being waged." When the club was raided women spoke to the press and provided McGuinness with damage control. Mrs. Conlon, his literary ally, became co-leader of the club and remained for many years a confidant. As early as 1929, McGuinness predicted the election of a female president.

One of the traditions that has died out in Greenpoint is the political parade. Club members loved the many marches they took part in. One of the most memorable and largest events the club ever held was its reception of Mayor Hylan in his bid for re-election. Politicians like McGuinness boosted their standing in the mayor's eyes by turning people out for rallies, and on Thursday September 3, 1925, McGuinness wowed Mayor Hylan who was on a campaign swing of North Brooklyn. Hylan finished an appearance in the Northside and met McGuinness outside the Carroll Club on Bedford Avenue. There was a big parade of Greenpoint cars with a flatbed truck that had a band on the bed of the truck. Cars all had placards on them saying, "Keep Honest Hylan." When it reached the corner of Manhattan and Meserole Avenues, there was a surging crowd outside the club. The alderman leaped out of the seat of one of the cars in front of a huge, raucous crowd and in a bellowing voice introduced the Mayor to a din of cheers. Hylan was taken aback by the size of the crowd and the feverish enthusiasm of the reception. He entered the clubhouse to make a speech to a few hundred members jammed inside

Other men used the position of Democratic Leader to seek other offices, but McGuinness thought that true leadership meant running the ward. Like most politicians of his generation, McGuinness considered congressmen members of an inferior class. To him, the local bosses who picked the legislators and told them what to do were the real political elite, and congressmen were the men who, unable to make the grade as leaders themselves, served as legislative errand boys to the bosses. He could not understand the tendency of political bosses taking Congressional nominations for themselves. "I'd never be such a sap as to send meself to Washington", and he said, "Believe me, I'm glad I was never in a fix where anyone else could send me. I'm asking you, if a man's a leader in New York, what the hell business has he got being in Washington?"

McGuinness felt that one of the best ways for him to keep abreast of news in Greeenpoint was to walk the district. Once every week or two, he spent a whole day covering his district on foot, checking on garbage collection, playground administration, compliance with the tenement laws, the efficiency of the Fire and Police Departments, and the condition of the pavements. If he saw or heard of anything wrong—a stopped-up sewer, a hole in the pavement, or traffic on a play street, he got in touch with the appropriate authorities. Often he worked with his Irish nose. One of McGuinness' many boasts was that he has made Greenpoint smell better. He forced factory owners to install devices eliminating objectionable smells and smoke, and was constantly sniffing for new evidences of polluted air. As soon as he detected an unpleasant odor on the wind, he called the manager of the offending plant, threatening to drag him into court for violating a whole series of city ordinances. He would then report back to the club his discoveries on his walk and how he was rectifying these problems.

McGuinness' club kept its people engaged in numerous political activities. There were speeches, debates, elections, lectures, reports and resolutions that made the club a humming beehive most nights of the week. Most entertaining, though, were the pronouncements McGuinness himself made, and they were not only local, but also national and international. One of McGuinness' boasts was his claim to be the first American politician to condemn Adolph Hitler, saying the People's Regular Democratic club was the first political organization in the country to pass an anti-Hitler resolution in the form of a telegram to President von Hindenburg early in 1933, advising him to yield no further powers to Hitler and to take steps to assure his personal security. McGuinness said that his reading of the news from Germany had convinced him that Hitler was personally plotting the assassination of Hindenburg, and claimed to be certain that Hindenburg's death in 1934 was at Hitler's hand. "I knew all along what that one was up to," he said, "I'll go to me own grave knowing he killed the old gentleman."

McGuinness also claimed that he was prescient when it came to the technological revolution making many jobs obsolete. The writer Joseph Mitchell once told McGuinness that he wanted to interview him on the subject of technocracy. McGuinness did not understand the term, but once he grasped it, he grew animated and talked about local women employed in a pretzel factory whose jobs were made redundant by a new machine. He said that he was one of the first Cassandras of the dangers of automation and the machine age. He said:

> I seen it coming. Away back in 1928 I seen the machine age coming. One night in a club meeting I warned my constituents about the machine age. Technocracy is nothing new to me. So far as I know I was one of the first to talk about it.

The alderman looked at the dial on his telephone, and the sight made him angry. He said, "It's got so that everything is hooked up to a machine." Mitchell asked him if he had any ideas to prevent the danger of mechanization. McGuinness replied that he had, stating:

> Every machine the patent office down there in Washington puts their oak on will do away with the work of men. There ought to be a stop out on the work done by the Patent Office. Just notify them they can't o.k. any more of these new machines. We got to put a stop to the machine age and so far as I know that's the best way.

A great many of the members of the club joined because they believed that McGuinness could help their careers. One of the club members explained this aspect of the club. William Holwell explained the club's purpose in a 1929 speech, noting that Greenpoint had 1,500 city employees including a hundred and fifty cops, an equal number of teachers and a hundred sanitation workers. He said:

> All these men and women continually look to improve their standing. They seek advice for improvement. They need a helping hand that they must have someone to look for favor. They are entitled to it and the best means for it is to have one large gathering place, and in Greenpoint that club should be a Democratic one where all could come and be encouraged, especially the alien in our midst, who seeks American citizenship.

Though McGuinness helped people, he was above graft and expected others to be equally as honest. He had three pieces of advice for people he got jobs: first, pay attention to your job, second, don't let anyone give you a five-cent piece, and number three, stay honest. A few former officers of his club defected to McQuade's organization because there was no payoff involved in club membership. One of these defectors was the child of his co-leader. There was a messy scandal involving published accusations by Co-Leader Conlon's son, who alleged McGuinness of corruption. The allegation angered McGuinness greatly. The young Conlon got himself physically ejected from the club by McGuinness' brother George when he once tried to enter.

In 1928, the Club moved into its new and final home at 119 Norman Avenue. Of course, there was a huge celebration and the club was officially opened by James A. Farley, New York State's most important Democratic Party official, the political kingmaker responsible for Franklin D. Roosevelt's election as president. Farley's presence at the club opening seemed to be another sign of McGuinness' power, but an incident would occur in the building that would embarrass McGuinness and raise more questions about his connections to organized crime.

Chapter Twenty-Three: The Great Depression and the New Deal

In the late 1920s, few people suspected that America was on the verge of the greatest economic crisis in its history. Pete McGuinness, however, publically predicted that the prosperity would not last. On one night in October of 1929, a month before the great crash a hundred people showed up at his headquarters looking for some kind of work. He prophetically called the economic situation "false prosperity," and the crash the next month vindicated his analysis.

The Great Depression hit Greenpoint especially hard because the area was heavily dependent on industrial orders, which quickly dried up after the crash. Factories began massive layoffs and by some estimates fully one half of Greenpointers were out of work. The alderman railed against the inaction of the federal government by Herbert Hoover, and said that something had to be done quickly to help the country. He said, "Such conditions must be relieved. If it is not then I hesitate to predict what can reasonably be expected in the near future when hunger may incite these people to drastic acts. Charity today is a solemn duty we owe to our less fortunate neighbors." For McGuinness, the dire situation in the country was not an abstract notion, but a visible reality. "I came face to face with conditions of poverty. In Greenpoint there are more than a thousand people who are on the point of actual hunger."

The Depression made Greenpointers love aged Fr. McGolrick of St. Cecilia's Parish even more. McGolrick became a staunch ally of McGuinnes in the fight against local hunger. Although an old man, he preformed Herculean efforts to feed his many hungry parishioners. For many local families, the pastor was the only difference between life and death from starvation. In the years before the New Deal there was no welfare or any other kind of social program that could care for the indigent, especially when the breadwinner was out of work, as thousands were locally.

A reporter asked McGuinness to comment on a report that his district faced the worst poverty in the entire city. He responded, "God must have loved the poor people if he centered them all in Greenpoint. While my folks are poor they are honest. Why shouldn't the Garden Spot suffer? It is the second largest district for factories and industry in the country. Well the depression hit business and them places shut down, so with no work the people in Greenpoint are up agin it."

McGuinness supported any measures that would feed his hungry constituents. He became a strong advocate of a program advocated by Eleanor Roosevelt, then the first lady of New York State, called "Block Aid." The idea was that wealthier people would provide direct food assistance to the hungry. He said that there were six hundred needy families in Greenpoint who could be helped by the program.

Not surprisingly, McGuinness was an early supporter of Franklin D. Roosevelt and his New Deal program for federal intervention to end the Depression. McGuinness liked to think of himself as one of the architects of the New Deal. He asserted his claim by pointing to a series of resolutions he sponsored in 1922, which gave what he calls the "per dime" employees of the city paid holidays and sick leave. These measures, which were, of course, negations of the idea of per diem employment, were, he believed, forerunners of such legislation as the National Fair Labor Standards Act and the National Labor Relations Act. "When you look back on it," he said in 1946, "You can see I was working on a lot of them humane matters meself twenty-five years ago."

Greenpoint was the kind of area that the Democrats

had to win with big margins if they were to carry New York State and win the Electoral College, so Roosevelt campaigned there in 1932. McGuinness took him around Greenpoint. F.D.R saw Italian restaurants and barber shops, Polish social clubs, Jewish Candy shops and Greek lunch wagons, but finally he asked Pete, "Where are the signs of your people, the Irish in Greenpoint?" Pete replied, "Well Governor, there are not many Irish left. Most of them now are dead and in Calvary Cemetery." A tense silence ensued and Roosevelt feared he had said something wrong, but suddenly McGuinness shot up his head and stated, "Don't worry, Governor you will still hear from all of them dead Irish on Election Day." Roosevelt rolled up huge majorities in Greenpoint on route to the presidency. In thanks, McGuinness was invited to Washington for the inauguration and was slated to march in the inaugural parade, but he sprained his ankle and had to watch from the reviewing stand. It was the beginning of a long and warm friendship between Roosevelt and McGuinnness.

The Depression decimated the budget of the City of New York. Drastic cuts had to be made. Even the eloquence and charm of McGuinness could not save the Greenpoint Ferry, which for years prior to the Depression had been a target for the budget axe. In 1933 the City announced that the ferry would cease service. The melancholy event was noted in *The Weekly Star* by Anon:

THE OLD FERRY

Ay, tear her tattered ensign down
For fifty years it's flown
And many a heart in Greenpoint
Will raise a heartfelt moan.
Upon her decks on many a morn
The crowds have rushed to work,
To reach Manhattan's dingy isle
In fog or rain or murk

Her pilot oft has gripped the wheel
To breast the river's tide,
While Pete McGuinness, glad, looked on
It was his greatest pride.

On many a summer's evening
It took the kids in tow,
The little ones of Greenpoint
Who had no place else to go.

O better that her aged hulk
Should ne'er be seen again
Brave Peter fought to save it

But all alas in vain.

Dry-dock her somewhere down the stream
And strip her to the keel.
You can't imagine anyhow
How sad the people feel.

McGuinness was on hand to see the ferry's final sailing. Deeply saddened, he read Walt Whitman's "Crossing Brooklyn Ferry" and then made the claim that Whitman was actually writing not about the Fulton Street Ferry, but the Greenpoint Ferry. He said, "Whitman sung about that ferry and when I say sung I mean he wrote a poem about it." Reading a stanza or two out of the Whitman poem, which sings of the sea gulls oscillating their bodies, the tall masts of Manhattan and the beautiful hills of Brooklyn, he continued, "If that wasn't wrote about the Greenpoint line I don't know what it was. And they're taking it away, I mean the ferry." *The Brooklyn Daily Eagle* noted that when the ferry departed for its final journey there was a tear in McGuinness' eye.

James Farley, chosen Postmaster General by Roosevelt and still head of the Democratic Party, was a fan of McGuinness. Farley and McGuinness developed a warm friendship. McGuinness treasured a cigarette case that Farley had given him. When Farley heard that the autographed picture he gave the district leader had been stolen from McGuinness' desk, he immediately sent him another one. Farley, however, rewarded his friend McGuinness in an even more unprecedented way. He allowed McGuinness, who was then sheriff of Brooklyn, to speak at the 1936 Democratic National Convention, an honor usually bestowed on senators or congressmen, not sheriffs. He said that the most memorable moment of his life came when Farley asked him to read, over a national radio hookup, the resolution thanking the networks for their coverage. "Bejesus," he said, "I stood up there on the platform with the vice-president of the United States of America, Honorable John Nance Garner, behind me, and senators, and cabinet members, and governors from the states that are Democratic, and I talked to the whole goddam United States. Me nerves were all jumping. I was cold all over. I'm telling you, you could see the sweat roll down me back. Right then, me whole life passed before me eyes."

During the 1936 Presidential campaign, Franklin D. Roosevelt spoke in Greenpoint. Before he was introduced, he confided in McGuinness that he was troubled by the *Literary Digest* straw vote, in which Governor Alfred M. Landon, the Republican candidate, was well in the lead. "That was one of me very biggest moments," McGuinness says. "I told him, I said, "Mr. President, don't you go giving it another thought. I got that goddam fake figured out." The president asked McGuinness what he meant. McGuinness explained that he had recently assigned three reliable members of the Greenpoint People's Regular Democratic Organization to spy on the city incinerator in the district. Some constituents who lived near the incinerator had complained that horses were being cremated there. They were certain they had detected the stink of burning horseflesh. The McGuinness followers spent three nights hiding in some bushes near the plant to see if horses were being cremated there, and they discovered that every night, after the Sanitation Department trucks had dumped their loads, some men known to be Republican party workers were coming in and buying up stacks of paper. Closer snooping showed that they were collecting discarded *Literary Digest* ballots. "Mr. President," McGuinness said to Roosevelt, "The people of Brooklyn get them fake ballots, and they throw them right out. The Republicans go to the incinerator and buy them for a nickel a piece. That's why Landon's ahead." Roosevelt laughed. Later in the campaign, he sent word to McGuinness, through Jim Farley, that he was no longer worrying about the straw vote. "He thanked me for relieving his brain." McGuinness said. "Bejesus, you feel good when you do a thing like that."

Even though Roosevelt was extremely busy, he stayed

aware of McGuinness' support. In 1936, Al Smith, the unsuccessful Democratic nominee for president in 1924, felt betrayed by Roosevelt and famously turned his back on FDR, beginning to attack the New Deal publically. McGuinness suggested a debate between Smith and his old friend Mayor Jimmy Walker, an ardent Roosevelt supporter, in Prospect Park. The idea so amused the President that he sent McGuinness a handwritten note from the White House:

> I have just read with delight your suggestion for a joint debate. While the idea is an excellent one, I hope that if it is finally arranged to hold the discussion in Prospect Park as was suggested that the crowd can be accommodated without chopping down all the trees.
>
> Very Sincerely Yours,
>
> Franklin Roosevelt.

The Roosevelts appreciated the huge margins of Democratic votes McGuinness delivered for F.D.R. Eleanor Roosevelt raised McGuinness' prestige even higher when she became the first American first lady to speak in support of striking workers. In 1941, the first lady came to speak in Greenpoint on behalf of the strikers at the Leviton Plant on Greenpoint Avenue who were demanding collective bargaining and a fifteen-cent an hour raise. Years later, when Roosevelt was elected to his final term in 1944, McGuinness sent the very ill president a congratulatory telegram. Despite the fact that Roosevelt had the immense task of being commander-in-chief responsible for winning the Second World War, he again sent McGuinness a hand written note from the White House that read:

> Dear Peter,
>
> Thank you very much indeed for your letter of congratulations. You know, of course. How much I appreciate your loyal support.
>
> Franklin Delano Roosevelt

Roosevelt had less than a year to live; McGuinness did not have long to live either.

Chapter Twenty-Four: More Questions

In the early 1930s, the furor surrounding McGuinness' arrest on gambling charges had subsided, yet larger questions about his rule remained. Greenpoint had a long and proud tradition of insurgents defying bosses and seizing power, just as McGuinness himself had done a decade earlier. Some locals believed McGuinness had become corrupt, as a mountain of circumstantial evidence suggested, and they called for a revolt against him.

One of McGuinness' greatest achievements as a legislator was his forcing the city to route the new crosstown subway line through Greenpoint, but even this success would raise questions about McGuinness. In 1930, after decades of waiting, the city announced plans for construction of the new line. McGuinness declared to great fanfare a Sunday parade down Manhattan Avenue on March 2, 1930 to celebrate the announcement, but McGuinness forgot that the police did not authorize Sunday parades. McGuinness publicized the parade everywhere, but could not use even his considerable pull to get a Sunday parade in violation of city ordinances prohibiting Sunday nonreligious marches. McGuinness was in the embarrassing position of having to cancel the parade for lack of a permit. Ten thousand disappointed people, according to his enemies, waited in vain for the subway parade.

His enemies pounced on the error. McQuade dubbed him "Paradeless Pete" and harped on the crowds of people waiting for hours along Manhattan Avenue for the canceled event. McQuade related with glee how when his rival finally did come, he jumped up on a table and announced there would be no parade. "What a hero!" said McQuade sarcastically. however, McQuade would increase the mockery by asking James McCarthy, the Bard of Greenpoint, to write a comic verse in the local paper about Paradeless Pete. He wrote:

Pete's Big Parade

They were four by four maybe fifty more
Waiting for the subway parade.
There was the D.S.C band who looked so grand
Waiting for the big parade.
There were mothers and sisters

And on their feet were blisters.
Gee what a sacrifice they made.

In their eyes there were tears
When it came to their ears
That there'd be no parade.

They gathered round at the breaking of ground
Near the start of Pete's parade.
The mayor was to be there,
But he gave it the air
Because Pete's permit was stayed.

The crowd was waiting, Pete was hesitating
Gee what a leader he has made.
Now if you want to win, just cast your vote for Jim
And he will soon have a big parade.

McGuinness had always denied charges leveled at him that he knew of bootlegging and organized crime. He knew it existed, but simply preferred to turn a blind eye to it. However, a police raid would create serious doubts about McGuinness' veracity.

On June 23, 1928, six members of the police "Strong Arm Squad" entered McGuinness' club, "The Veteran's Labor League," on Greenpoint Avenue and ransacked the place. This was the very same "Confidential Squad" that had attacked his club the previous year. Local veterans ran the club, which McGuinness had started during his days in "The Greenpoint Patriotic League." The attacking officers at first seemed to victimize heroic local war veterans. McGuinness, with his usual flare for publicity, sought to make political capital out of the attack, showing the press how the police had smashed pictures of Theodore Roosevelt and General John Pershing. The cops also broke a clock and, according to McGuinness, stole $32 intended for wreaths of dead soldiers. McGuinness claimed that the six attackers made no arrests, but did a thousand dollars worth of damage. When one of the club veterans who had suffered a bayonet wound in the back in France resisted, McGuinness claimed that a gun was stuck into his ribs. McGuinness announced that he was contemplating suing the city and he stated, "This crowd has been getting away with this stuff for too long in Greenpoint. They've entered other places that were conducted within the law, smashed things up and gotten away with it without anyone complaining, but I am going to force a showdown this time."

Again a police raid caused major embarrassment to McGuinness, who was invited to police headquarters to discuss the raid. Police Commissioner Whalen showed him evidence proving the club was a hangout for ex-cons, gunmen and beer runners, and Whalen shared his proof of racketeers using the club with the press. Again, McGuinness's reputation for honesty was thrown into doubt. McGuinness had to eat his words and publically apologize. McGuinness claimed he was "taken in" by being made honorary president. He added apologetically, "After looking at the records I am perfectly satisfied with what the police did. I will never protect gangsters and criminals. I never did and I never will, if I never hold another office in my life." *The Brooklyn Daily Eagle* opined, "McGuinness is the fighting type of politician, yet he is learning that when you are manifestly in the wrong the best thing is to own up, apologize and forget it, if possible."

Former Police Chief Enright rubbed salt in McGuinness' fresh wounds. The ex-commissioner said that the incident in the club was connected to "Little Augie Carfano," an associate of the notorious gangster Al Capone. Enright claimed that McGuinness was well aware of Carfano's involvement in the club and that McGuinness' protestations of ignorance were nothing more than evasiveness.

McGuinness would suffer one more embarrassing incident. On New Year's Eve the authorities raided a restaurant in the basement of his political clubhouse at 119 Norman Avenue and staff members were arrested for running a speakeasy. The papers and many people in Greenpoint asked incredulously how McGuinness could be unaware that a speakeasy was operating directly under his club. A dark cloud seemed to be forming over McGuinness' head and circumstantial evidence pointed to his collusion with criminal elements. The local politician and poet James McCarthy, "The Bard of Greenpoint," challenged McGuinness and ran against him for district leader. He accused McGuinness of "Czarism" and claimed that the district leader was trying to "Russianize Greenpoint." Worst of all though, were the catchy ditties he wrote about the leader, "First of all the floppers was he who sung of Greenpoint harmony. For fifteen years he has won, but what has he ever done?"

In another verse he attacked the regal nature of McGuinness Greenpoint rule:

> Old King McGuinness was a very old blade,
> A merry old blade he was
> He ruled his domain with might and main,
> As proud as a king could be. No matter how old or wise,
> His despotic reign gave the people pain, and opened up their eyes.
> The people's voice renounced his choice

> They say now Mr. Smarty independent, we shall always be
> And vote for James McCarthy.

Finally, the people of Greenpoint learned in 1930, that New York State had announced plans for a special committee to investigate corruption in New York City. The Hofstadter Commission would investigate local politicians who had run afoul of the law and they would subpoena both McQuade and McGuinness, whose enemies relished the idea of seeing the big district leader being grilled under oath about his ties to illegal gambling. McGuinness' enemies delighted in imaging the grammar school dropout wilting under interrogation by Judge Seabury, a staunch Republican and an enemy of both Democrats and corruption. It seemed highly likely McGuinness would compromise himself under oath and his political career in Greenpoint would end. They eagerly awaited the spectacle of McGuinness' testimony.

Chapter Twenty-Five: Vindication

New York State Governor Franklin Roosevelt, intending to run for president in 1932, feared attack for allowing the rampant political corruption in New York City. To blunt this accusation, he approved the creation of a special legislative investigation, the Hofstadter Committee, also known as the Seabury Investigations, which was a joint legislative committee formed by the New York State Legislature to investigate corruption in New York City. Prime among its targets were Registrar McQuade and District Leader McGuinness. The chairman of the commission was State Senator Samuel H. Hofstadter, but the actual investigations were carried out by Ex-Judge of the Court of Appeals Samuel Seabury, who was appointed legal counsel to the committee. At that time it was the largest investigation of municipal corruption in American history.

The investigations would destroy many of the Tammany Hall politicians of the day. McGuinness' old friend, Mayor Jimmy Walker, was forced to resign for his inability to account for more than seven hundred thousand dollars stashed in a bank account. At first, Walker denied the money was his, but he finally admitted owning it, although Walker could not explain how he amassed such a fortune. In 1932, the mayor resigned in shame. Seabury and his staff also subpoenaed the bank accounts of Tammany Hall legislators and found that collectively lawmakers had stashed away millions of dollars. McGuinness' old nemesis from the Board of Alderman, Thomas Farley, had $40,000 stashed away in a "wonderful box." After being exposed by Seabury, the papers called him "Tin Box Farley" and, his reputation for honesty tarnished, his career in politics was doomed.

One of the chief targets of the investigation was Registrar McQuade. An investigation of his bank accounts revealed that in six-and-a-half years he had deposited more than a half million dollars, while failing to file income tax during many of those years. Seabury asked the registrar to explain how such a large sum appeared in his bank account. McQuade said that he had borrowed the money because he was the sole means of support for thirty-four family members. He said, "When the family business was liquidated the thirty-four McQuades were placed on my back. I being the only breadwinner and after that it was necessary to keep life in their bodies and sustenance to go out and borrow money." The judge inquired to recall the names of the people who had given him such large sums of money. "Well Mr. Registrar, will you be good enough to indicate from whom you borrowed the money?" "Oh Judge, offhand I could not," McQuade replied.

Seabury asked what the people were doing in his club when the police raided it. McQuade replied that the people in his club were there for his library. When they searched his library they could not find any books and the main periodical in his library was *Armstrong's Scratch Sheet*. Among literary elements in the work were the names of racehorses: Phillip the First, Parley, Faithful Friend and Sir Maurice. McQuade admitted he regularly bailed out gamblers, but only as a beneficial act of friendship for friends and neighbors.

The newspapers pilloried McQuade and dubbed his needy relatives "the thirty-four starving McQuades." The revelations of the huge sums in his account and his evasiveness in answering Seabury spelled the end of his political career. He became a public laughing stock and would never again challenge McGuinness.

McGuinness was scheduled to testify the following day, realizing that his political future was also in danger. If the papers presented him in the same corrupt light as McQuade, his political career was through. The shrewdest course of action would have been to use the Fifth Amendment right to remain silent, but McGuinness waived that right, wanting to clear his good name. Unlike many of the other witnesses who appeared before Seabury, McGuinness would answer all the questions directly and not plead the fifth.

McGuinness' candid strategy was a risky one. Seabury had already embarrassed many politicians during the hearings and ruined their careers. When people compared the eloquent ex-State Supreme Court justice with the plain speaking grammar school graduate from Greenpoint, even many of McGuinness' most ardent supporters feared that Seabury in cross-examination would make mincemeat of McGuinness.

On October 13, 1931, his political career hanging in the balance, McGuinness, waiving his rights to immunity, agreed to answer the ex-judge's questions. McGuinness came accompanied by a crowd of dozens of Greenpointers in his usual high spirits. Striding briskly to the witness stand, he signed the waiver with a flourish. "Gentlemen," he said to the attending members of the Hofstadter Committee, "I am glad to present me presence here today Judge," The judge asked him about his rise to power in Greenpoint and how he had managed to take the leadership away from someone with as much family support as McQuade. He responded, "I did not take it away. The people of my district took it away and they gave it to me." He asked McGuinness why he had named himself as assistant commissioner of public works. His answer was classic: "Well, I couldn't suggest a more better person for the job than myself."

Seabury brought up the gambling incident and asked McGuinness if he accepted full responsibility for it. "Your Honor," McGuinness said, "There's only one leader of that club. Right here before you. Shoot, Judge." McGuinness had said in a pre-hearing deposition that he had only allowed gambling in his club because his rival McQuade had card games that were drawing political supporters across the street to McQuade's club.

McGuinness informed Seabury that the first time he had learned that professionals were using his club as a base of operations was from Borough Leader McCoey at his office in February 1927, and that he had determined to find out if the accusations were true. McGuinness explained that he was only in the club on the night of the raid to determine the truth of McCoey's accusations. He had determined to be his own detective and secreted himself in a dark part of his club behind a pillar, observing what transpired there. Seabury asked him with mock surprise if he was really spying on the members of his own club. McGuinness replied, "Yes, I would spy on them too. Don't forget that."

McGuinness revealed that he learned that five members of the club were professional gamblers. He said that he assembled them in his office, telling them that McCooey had informed him about the police charges. He then told them, "If this goes on you are going to be in a lot of trouble and don't think I'm going to stand for it. Now if this ain't cut out, it's up to yourselves."

Seabury then asked him if he agreed with the police regarding wrongdoing at his club. McGuinness reply became legendary. He said, "Judge in all my public life me and the police never agreed on anything." His response sent the room in paroxysms of laughter.

Seabury then referred to Alderman "Tin Box" Farley, I looked all over for your tin box and could not find it." McGuinness replied, "Here, Judge is the only tin box I own: my wallet. It's been my safe for twelve years. "There's nothing more safer than if you've got it in your pocket." He added," This is me Jewish Mezuzah. It's filled with all my neighbors troubles." The wallet that McGuinness produced was a foot long and many times larger than the size of a normal man's wallet and was fully the size of a horse's feedbag.

McGuinness thundered, "I'll be a good fellow; I'll open it for you." The judge declined and banged his gavel, but McGuinness ignored him and reached into a compartment, pulling out his father-in- law's button, which he proffered to the judge. "He was a great Champeen your honor." The Greenpointers in the audience laughed hysterically and McGuinness seemed more court jester than witness under interrogation.

Seabury inquired whether he was accurately quoted as saying "Here comes the police, cheese it." Pete corrected him saying, "No Your Honor, I said, Cheese it! Here comes the cops," even somber Judge Seabury could not contain his laughter.

Seabury asked him about the safe in his club and the huge amounts of cash it contained. "Judge I don't know anything about it," McGuinness swore, raising his right hand. McGuinness claimed that he had nothing in the safe, not even a toothpick and that he did not even know the combination to the safe in his own office. He said that any member of the club could use the safe.

Seabury asked about the $8,000 in profit that was in the safe: "Doesn't that suggest to you that the club got some of the $8,000 profit?" "I do not know," said Pete, evincing his first signs of uneasiness. Seabury asserted that the over $8,000 in winnings was pretty good profits. "Corking profits," replied McGuinness. Seabury then asked, "Who accounts for this money that comes in?" "Not me," answered McGuiness. He continued, "If it was $9,000 or $10,000 profit it didn't mean nothing to me, nothing to Peter McGuinness."

Seabury wanted details about the financial books of his club, but again McGuinness was evasive, stating, "I could never answer that question. I never familiarize myself with that." McGuinness mentioned that the treasurer kept the books at home, which made Seabury incredulous. McGuinness responded, "Sometimes the club members would start a little rough and tumble stuff at the club and if they kept the books there, away would go all our records." Seabury incredulously asked if his own club members would actually throw the financial books around the club. "If one or two was fooling they would pick up the book and hit the other with it." "And damage the financial records?" asked the judge.

"Absolutely" McGuinness replied. The Commission had investigated McGuinness' bank accounts and although there were a few minor irregularities with his account, such as co-mingling of funds, McGuinness' records showed that he had not amassed the kinds of large sums that the other politicians under investigation had collected. He had no huge stash of cash like his archrival McQuade.

McGuinness asserted that there was no proof that professional gambling was going on in his club, and McGuinness claimed on the stand, "I have never gambled in my life and I do not know anything about it. But just suppose someone who is a member of the club comes in there and starts to make a book. What do they want me to do? Throw him out?" Seabury asked the district leader if he were not responsible for the actions in his club. McGuinness responded, "If a man murders another man I hope that they do not arrest McGuinness."

Seabury then inquired, "But didn't you resent being arrested?" McGuinness turned his head to the ceiling and with a look of great agitation and bellowed, "The whole world knows that."

Seabury asked McGuinness to describe the charitable activities of his club. McGuiness perked up and said, "Judge you're doing me a great and wonderful favor." McGuiness told the judge about the Christmas baskets and other club charities with gusto. He said, "I have dug down in my own pockets more times in history that any leader of the county or the state." The judge then implied that profits from gambling had funded the charities, and McGuinness grew both tired and indignant. McGuinness said, "Judge bury it. It is dead. Don't be talking about it any more. (I am) "tired of looking at it." Seabury ended his line of questioning.

At the end of his testimony, Seabury told him that it gave him great pleasure to give him back his savings book, to which McGuinness responded, "It has been a pleasure gentlemen, coming before you. I want to thank Mr. Seabury too for being so kind and courteous to me."

McGuinness swept off the stand. Later, Seabury was asked why he kept McGuinness on the stand for six long hours. He replied, "because I liked to hear him talk."

McGuinness had not only survived the hearing, but he had also brilliantly defended his reputation for honesty and high comedy. He was one of the very few politicians who emerged from the investigation with his reputation enhanced. He had vindicated himself and proven his honesty. He became one of the few remaining elder statesmen in Brooklyn, and increasingly the papers consulted him any time that they wanted his unique and amusing insights into political, social and even historic questions. He would soon become one of the most loved figures in Brooklyn and would parley that love into countywide office.

Chapter Twenty-Six: Celebrations

No leader in American history ever celebrated with more gusto than McGuinness. Looking back, he recalled, "Almost every time we'd get a new lamppost, we'd have ourselves a parade." Practically every local civic and religious organization marched in these celebrations, often accompanied by marching bands. Everybody paraded, even McQuade and the handful of Republicans in Greenpoint. McGuinness' club members were usually first in the line of march, just behind Professor Connolly's band. "The parades was at night," he said, "and the horses wasn't working then, so we thought it would be nice to have them in the parades." McGuinness often led the parades mounted on a white truck horse and wearing a 10-gallon hat. Many of these celebrations happened during the worst years of the Depression, but Greenpoint celebrated, seemingly in defiance of the gloom that permeated the country.

Perhaps McGuinness' greatest celebrations marked the opening of the cross-town subway line. For a quarter century Greenpoint had been trying to get a subway line. Originally the line was not planned to go through Greenpoint, but when McGuinness learned of this affront to the area, he bellowed the legendary question, "What is Greenpoint, Siberia?" His friend Jimmy Walker promised that the construction of the line that became the G train would begin in Greenpoint, but the Mayor's scandal and subsequent resignation killed that promise.

When announcement of the line was made in 1930, McGuinness' inability to get a parade permit was the cause of embarrassment. He became the butt of jokes by the McQuade camp as "Paradeless Pete," but finally in August of 1933, the line was ready and McGuinness could enjoy his triumph.

McGuinness had a strong sense that this was a historic occasion and he wanted the oldest living people born in the area to lead the festivities. Mrs. John Bell, who was eighty-three years old and born in 1850, was the ceremonial engineer on the first train that ran through the station. Also aboard was eighty one-year-old John Lockwood. They also lead the parade down Manhattan Avenue to commemorate the occasion. In old Greenpoint torch lit parades celebrated great events and McGuinness continued that tradition with three thousand marchers, in the subway ceremonies. Between thirty thousand and fifty thousand onlookers watched, and more than a hundred local organizations would march in the parade.

John O'Loughlin, a retired Brooklyn politician turned newspaper reporter knew the best place to experience the parade was right next to Alderman Peter J. McGuinness, who pronounced the line's opening the happiest day of his life and was in grand form to celebrate.

O'Loughlin found McGuinness at about ten-thirty —right before the start of the parade. He had to wade through a sea of civic organizations—the boy scouts, girl scouts and some group of children right in front of Pete all clad in kelly green jackets. Pete was, of course, with his group "The Greenpoint People's Regular Democratic Club, along with its band. Pete's club, numbering about three hundred marchers stood seven or eight abreast. All the members of the club carried American flags, and they were vocal with joy as they formed into ranks to start the march. Pete marched with a stately gait with his chin up and he carried the stars and stripes across his shoulders like a musket borne by a soldier.

Around Clay Street, a woman cried, "There's Pete, aint he wonderful!," and Pete immediately lost the stiff dignified pose that he had just been marching with. He turned to the crowd, and a big gleaming smile lit up his face. He waved the flag in her direction, for he knew her.

He cried out, "Hey Maggie how ya doin'?" Suddenly, a big roar went up from the crowd, and everyone began to cheer. Pete, ever the gentleman, was forced to take his hat off with his left hand, while he carried the standard with his right.

There were greetings on every side and the parade soon turned into a demonstration for Pete. O'Loughlin remarked sarcastically, "They seem to know you," to which Pete replied, "I could tell you all their first names." As the parade reached Greenpoint Avenue, there was such a throng of viewers that the line of march was broken up by the crowd pressing forward, and after the parade crossed the avenue there was no longer any decent order. The crowds began to recognize Pete in greater numbers and they shouted in greater volume. O'Loughlin began to wonder if the roar was really for the subway, or if it was really for Pete.

As the parade reached St. Anthony's, a runner came up to Pete from his band and asked him so inaudible question. Pete answered in the affirmative and suddenly the band began to play Adeste Fidelis, the Christmas tune. A whole army of spectators began to sing it, as did almost all the marchers in that section of the parade. Everyone seemed to know all the words, and the men in line seemed to keep step to the tune.

A few minutes later, the band began to play the Irish

air "Killkenny." Pete suddenly forgot that he was leading a column in a parade, for the lilt of the music got into his Irish blood, and Pete began to dance a kind of jig. The on-looking crowd roared with approval, and they shouted Pete's name while they danced in unison with him while they sang:

> It's there they spend their money freely
> And of all the towns in Ireland Killkenny is for me.

The shouts, singing and music were all so contagious that Pete marched along with a kind of dance step until the band played a more somber tune.

> When the march reached the RKO Theater on the corner of Calyer and Manhattan, the title of the film they were showing was "How I love That Man" and O'Loughlin couldn't help but think that it referred to Pete.

O'Loughlin studied the faces. It was the old-time enthusiasm of old-time Greenpoint, which hadn't changed in thirty years. They were all neighbors who knew the men and women in line and certainly recognized their leader. He made a mental note that other sections had changed, newer elements had come in and completely overrun or even obliterated the old landmarks, but Greenpoint was still Greenpoint-the same rugged types as years ago, the same love of excitement, of the marching parades, of the music and the bands and of all the hurrah that went with the torchlight demonstrations of the past. Above all, was the fanatical devotion to their leader-a man whom the community idolized and cheered on every public occasion.

As they swung into the circle around the speaker's stand at Nassau Avenue, O'Loughlin asked himself the question: will this new subway change Greenpoint? He thought of the rush of new population that was sure to come and of the construction of large apartments that were sure to be built. He also thought of the subtle, but sure metamorphosis that usually follows great civic improvements and, amidst all the joy of the celebration, he felt one pang of regret, for he loved old Greenpoint just as it was.

Another major local celebration was the hundredth birthday of Mary Logan on June 23, 1934, who lived at seventy seven DuPont Street. Mrs. Logan had lived a long, happy and peaceful life within the confines of three Greenpoint blocks. When she first arrived in Greenpoint from Ireland in 1859 at the age of 21, the district was a farming community and "Little more than a wilderness." She was quoted as saying that "There was not a pavement and hardly a well. We had to go to India St. for a pail of water... There was a beautiful orchard between Norman and Nassau Streets on Newell St., and many beautiful gardens." She even recalled a time when mothers commonly bathed their babies in the East River.

They would close the street and organize a monster block party for Mrs. Logan. Dozens of families helped prepare for the festivities, and many of the members of her parish, Ascension Church, also came out to celebrate. Houses were decorated with an array of lights, streamers and bunting. Porches were also decorated with Irish and American flags, and a congratulatory letter was read from President Franklin Roosevelt. The entire street was roped off, and hundreds of her neighbors celebrated in the street with her, including McGuinnness, who made a warm congratulatory speech explaining that he had first met her as a child and had known her all his life.

Logan was the mother of eight surviving children and there were five generations of her family present. She sat in a "throne-like" chair, and the large throng assembled in front of her house serenaded her. She had become feeble now, but her mind was clear, and she waved an American flag to the loud shouts of her celebrating neighbors. The celebration was even covered in *The New York Times*.

For years McGuinness had tried to get a pool for the neighborhood. Too many local kids had drowned swimming in the dangerous waters of The East River or Newtown Creek, but for years the City of New York had denied funding for the pool. However, during the Depression and The New Deal federal efforts would make the pool a reality.

One of the most joyous days in McGuinness' life was July 31, 1936, when the McCarren Park Pool was finally opened. Seventy-five thousand people showed up for the celebration, and the crowd was so large that special amplifiers had to be set up so that all the people could her the ceremonies. McGuinness had fought for a neighborhood pool since his first days as alderman, and now finally his dream was coming to fruition. The huge pool on Lorimer Street Between Driggs Avenue and Bayard Street was built with labor from Roosevelt's Works Progress Administration and was in all likelihood payback from Roosevelt and Farley for his work in turning out huge numbers of Democratic presidential votes for F.D.R.

The McCarren Park structure was more than a mere pool. It was a giant structure and a thing of beauty. The building's vast scale and dramatic arches, designed by Aymar Embury II, typified the generous and heroic spirit of New Deal architecture. The pool could accommodate six thousand eight hundred swimmers and measured an enormous three hundred and thirty feet by one hundred and sixty- five feet.

As usual in Greenpoint, a big parade celebrated the occasion, as McGuinness and the Mayor marched together. The pool was dedicated in a speech by McGuinness' old friend Mayor LaGuardia, who recognized McGuinness as the visionary behind the pool and recalled that sixteen years ago when they both served on the Board of Alderman, McGuinness had first proposed the pool. The mayor spoke of his old friend, calling him, "The Prince of the Garden Spot." Again, McGuinness declared the day the happiest of his life.

The subway line, the pool and other improvements proved that McGuinness' promises were not empty. He had made government work for the people and produced tangible results. However, the Depression was far from over, and the world soon be plunged into world war, which would end such great Greenpoint celebrations.

Chapter Twenty-Seven: Civic Virtue

In 1934, for the first time in fifteen years, McGuinness did not hold a city job. He was planning a campaign to become the sheriff of Brooklyn, and he needed an issue to get his name back in the press. A weird-looking, controversial statue standing in front of City Hall would catapult McGuinness' name back into the papers and provide Greenpoint with a lot of laughs.

Civic Virtue Triumphant Over Unrighteousness, (1909-22) was a huge bronze sculpture group and fountain designed by Brooklyn-born sculptor Frederick William MacMonnies. The 17-foot high sculpture portrayed a heroic-sized male nude, "Civic Virtue" with sword on shoulder, standing above two writhing female figures—the sirens of "Vice" and "Corruption." The sirens, with the heads and torsos of women and the tails of serpents, could not capture the man, and were caught in their own nets. The sculpture was mounted on a square pedestal adorned with dolphin heads that spewed water into basins at its sides.

The fountain and sculpture group were originally placed in front of New York City Hall in Manhattan by Mayor McClellan in 1909, but from the start the artwork created controversy and attracted intense criticism. Many objected on aesthetic grounds. They thought the central male figure flabby and unartistic. Others objected on moral grounds because the central figure was a nude. Many women found the sculpture misogynistic and called it " the Rough Guy" because they disliked the male figure stamping on the females' heads. LaGuardia hated the pudgy male and called the figure "the Fat Guy." He agreed with Parks Commissioner Robert Moses that it should be moved somewhere, but where?

A lot of people hated the sculpture, but not McGuinness. He loved the figure and the theme it represented. Instead of calling it "the Fat Guy" as the Mayor had done, he called it "the Tough Guy." He noticed that it had a marked resemblance to himself. He said, "It was almost as if I had posed for the statue myself." *The New York Times* agreed and remarked that some reports said that McGuinness, a man of gargantuan size, had posed for the statue. However, McGuinness denied the rumor about the nude figure and a quickly added that if he had posed for the statue, he would have worn a lumber carrier's apron.

Being on close personal terms with the mayor, he asked for the statue to be moved to McCarren Park in Greenpoint; the mayor initially approved Peter's request because he wanted the ugly piece of art out of sight, but this only created a firestorm of protest and a ton of free publicity for McGuinness.

McGuinnness claimed the statue in Greenpoint because it was the city's last vestige of civic virtue. He gave an interview in which he described how the statue and fountain would grace McCarren Park, while noting that the statue's value of $60,000. He described how a landscape artist would surround the sculpture with trees and shrubs, just like parks he had seen in Florida. *The Brooklyn Daily Eagle* even created a mock picture when it grafted McGuinness' head onto the body of the sculpture, so certain were they of its imminent relocation to McCarren Park.

McGuinness was asked if the nudity in the statue would not offend sensibilities amongst his deeply Catholic constituents. McGuinness averred that Greenpoint would welcome the statue, and even if they did not he would have a huge pair of red flannels drape the figure.

However, no sooner had McGuinness spoken of the statue's relocation to his district than a host of other districts also laid claim to the statue. Some said that the stature belonged in the Bronx. Others said that Coney Island deserved the sculpture. The District Leader of Williamsburg also claimed his area was the ideal new home for the statue. Dr. Joshua Freeman said, "I consider Civic Virtue a great piece of art, and there is no section more deserving than Williamsburg, which has been given little from a civic standpoint. Here is a chance for the city to make amends." Bushwick's district leader, however, was not part of the frenzy to get the statue. James Tuomey said, "We're loaded up with enough statues in Bushwick now. In fact we've got a statue for just about everything that ever happened. Let McGuinness have it. The people in Greenpoint are not as modest as we are here. I am afraid that the people of Bushwick would not like so much nakedness."

Perhaps Tuomey saw something that McGuinness had overlooked: citizen outrage at the misogynistic message some saw in the statue. Andrew Cortez, a retired Greenpoint boxer who was so outraged by the lewd statue that he mounted a write-in campaign against McGuinness' leadership of the Democratic Party, proclaimed the statue an insult to Greenpoint womanhood and stated, "The men of this district love their women. They won't forget the slur on this section when McGuinness tried to bring the statue here."

The statue, and the swirling controversy around it, created a growing headache for the mayor. If he had given it to Pete and to Greenpoint, then he would have stirred up resentment and charges of favoritism. Finally the controversy was settled when the pretentious Municipal Arts Commission moved it to Manhattan's Foley Square. McGuinness took the floor in the Board of Aldermen and said sarcastically, "It is noteworthy that the Municipal Art Commission placed that Immortal piece of art, Civic Virtue, in such a heavenly retreat like Foley Square. I doff my hat to the Municipal Art Commission and may it have long health and pleasant dreams and may the sunshine always rest on its brow."

For a while, he girded his enormous stomach with a belt whose large silver buckle had "Civic Virtue" engraved upon it. The free publicity he received from the scandal helped him in his race for sheriff the following year.

Chapter Twenty-Eight: Continuity and Change

Winds of change were blowing across the Brooklyn political landscape during the 1930s. The damaging revelations of the Hofstadter Commission spelled an end to McQuade's ambitions to be Greenpoint Democratic District Leader. In 1932, Brooklyn County Leader McCooey bluntly told him that he had to capitulate and admit McGuinness's position as District Leader. The scene of McQuade's surrender one May evening was one of the most dramatic pieces of street theater ever acted out in Greenpoint. It was a magnificent occasion, as solemn and formal as the Japanese surrender to General MacArthur in Tokyo Bay. McQuade, with hundreds of his followers, met at the club and locked the front door for the last time. Then, with McQuade leading, they marched slowly, as if to a dirge, down the middle of Manhattan Avenue turning onto Norman Avenue to the McGuinness Club. McGuinness regally awaited them at the head of the flight of steps leading to the door. James Burns, the Borough President of Brooklyn, flanked by McCooey, now a McGuinness enthusiast. McQuade walked up the steps, and McGuinness stepped two paces forward to take his hand. He then turned around and led the vanquished registrar inside, where McGuinness, McCooey and Burns watched McQuade and the hundred followers sign the McGuinness Club roster and give the treasurer their first year's dues. When this was done, McGuinness and McQuade went back to the clubhouse steps, in front of a large cheering crowd. Each made a brief address. "Peter J. McGuinness," McQuade said, "is now the undisputed leader of this district. Let no man say I am not earnest in my admiration of him. These ugly rumors must stop." McGuinness said, "From this day forward, Pete McGuinness and Jim McQuade march forward hand in hand like brothers for the benefit of the grand old Democratic Party."

McQuade had a little over three years to live. When he passed away McGuinness was magnanimous. In one of his speeches during the feud, he had said of McQuade, "He is the most despicable man in public life today. He is a man who is not even a man among men," but when McQuade died in 1935, McGuinness delivered a eulogy saying, "You could always say of old Jim McQuade that he was a man among men."

Roosevelt's New Deal had also dealt a mortal blow to political patronage. The federal government, not local politicians, now controlled many jobs. Ward bosses and the Democratic Party had far fewer plums to give out, and voters were killing many of the political jobs they once held. Mayor LaGuardia and the Fusion Party convinced New Yorkers to support ballot initiatives that did away with the very kinds of political positions that allowed career politicians like McGuinness to remain on city payrolls.

McGuinness opposed the reforms his friend LaGuardia advocated, feeling that his real service to society was the one he performed as a political leader in Greenpoint, and regarding being on the municipal payroll merely as a technical device to allow him to continue as ward boss. "The thing of it is," he said thoughtfully, "you got to make jobs like this so a political man can get his work done. If I was still in a lumberyard or if I was in a factory, I wouldn't have time to run Greenpoint." The Citizens Union disapproved of him and of his attitude and felt that he had no right to be at the public trough. "The record clearly indicates that he is not qualified for any public office," it declared each time he sought one. McGuinness did not take this seriously. "They mean I ain't a Republican," he said.

Brooklynites, though, were becoming more educated

and less reliant, as in days of old, on bosses and contracts. Increasingly middle-class Brooklynites did not need McGuinness or his machine. He explained the problem that education was creating: "The trouble with some people now is that they go to school and then go to college and do not understand neighborhoods. When you grow up with people in an overcrowded section you know everything they got to be going through. You know they have learned lessons on their mother's or father's knee that was never learned in any college." McGuinness had always been something of an anachronism, and after World War Two he was increasingly seen as a relic of the past.

McGuinness, though, was still a powerful figure with many friends, even in Washington. He had to use all his power to resist slum clearance. Unlike many other places in the city, no federal housing projects were erected in Greenpoint because McGuinness violently opposed them. Instead of condemning older housing and replacing it with new huge apartment blocks, McGuinness favored rehabilitating, not destroying, Greenpoint's existing housing stock. He saw the monstrous blocks as a threat to the area, defending the weather-beaten frame houses of his area as homes and allowing no government agency to condemn them.

Surprisingly, one of McGuinness's strongest supporters was the builder of government housing projects, Robert Moses, the power broker, whose diktats radically altered the city, destroying thousands of private homes. He said:

> It's absurd to expect a man like Peter to be an administrator. Peter is a leader and one of the best in the city. Call him a boss if you want I don't care. I've known him and worked with him for twenty years, and when ever I've needed to know anything about Greenpoint, I've got more practical help and cooperation from Peter than I could ever have got from a hundred social workers, sociologists, city planners, polltakers, and all the rest of that trash. No matter what you say about them, men like Peter have held New York's neighborhoods together, and if the reformers ever succeed in driving them out, take my word for it, this city is going to fall apart into racial and religious mobs. If you ask me, that's happening right now.

Even McGuinness' position as pitcher for the Board of Aldermen was changing. For years, even after McGuinness left the Board of Alderman, McGuinness pitched for the legislators with decidedly mixed, but highly comical results. McGuinness, however, learned that the Alderman no longer wanted him as pitcher. He wrote about it in a letter to Tim Sullivan, an alderman and a old friend from his days on the Board of Aldermen.

> Dear Timmy,
>
> A recent letter from Lew Haas has informed me roughly that I will not be able to pitch for my old Alma Mater, the Board of Aldermen, when they take the field July sixteenth. Say Timmy, this is outrageous! Where do they get this stuff from? Benching old Pete just when my fastball is hopping and my cure is winding around their necks. Is that gratitude? Now Timmy, I know these smart alleck aldermen that think that Pete is getting old. Those kids don't remember when I used to shut out the reporters with nineteen runs and forty-six hits. But we'll show em. I'll slap an injunction on them and pitch in spite of them and when my fastball roars up they'll be glad to let me pitch.

There was talk of ending the Board of Aldermen and replacing it with a new city legislative body. He foresaw the dangers of abolishing the Board of Aldermen, saying:

> The councilmen elected by proportional representation they aint responsible to no neighborhood. If you wanted the name of a street changed, why there was your alderman right there in the neighborhood and he filled your stocking at Christmas too and sent a bag of coal around when the flat got cold. Why dese Congressmen now I bet they got offices in Rockefeller Center. When there's anything to be done they are about as scarce as a Republican in Greenpoint.

In 1935, McGuinness ran for sheriff of Brooklyn against a fusion candidate, Harold Reynolds, who was supposedly representative of the new, more honest men who should run the city. McGuinness ran for borough-wide office for the first time in his career on a novel campaign promise of making life more agreeable for the prisoners under his care. He assured the voters that the prisoners in the county jail would be happy and well fed if he were elected. "Under me, they'll get better menus," he said in every speech. He was elected by the largest margin of victory of any sheriff in American history up until that time. Thousands of Greenpointers showed up at Borough Hall for his swearing in.

On his first day in office, he gave a New Year's party in the jail. He issued orders that hot drinks be passed around before bedtime, that beef stew be served no less than twice a week, and that carrots be served at least every other day. This last innovation made all the papers. McGuinness, who had a sure instinct for publicity, had called in the reporters and announced it himself. "Carrots is eye food," he said. "Mother of God, I figure we want them to be able to see the straight and narrow when we spring them." McGuinness won re-election, but his triumph was bittersweet. On the same ballot that elected him sheriff, voters in New York State voted to do away with his position as sheriff of Kings County. McGuinness would also become registrar, but again charter reform would abolish that position. It seemed that McGuiness' days in political offices were drawing to a close.

There was only one countywide job McGuinness ever said he wanted: McCooey's old post of county leader. He only once publicly disavowed any interest in the job. As a rule, he was indirect in answering reporters' questions. "I don't think I ought to be saying anything meself," he said last year, "but I will say for me sweetheart that it would make her proud as a bird of paradise." In1937, he made his one unequivocal statement: "The demands," he said to the press, reading slowly from a prepared statement, "have been so many and so general that after considerable thought and for the best interests of Greenpoint, I have decided to throw my hat in the ring and declare tonight that I am willing to accept this nomination should the county leader see fit to honor me."

The county leader, though, did not see fit because modern politicians required more education than McGuinness had. A man who called himself a "boss," as McGuinness freely and happily did, just wouldn't do, because it offended, everyone from the bar association to what McGuinness called "The Reverend Clergy." His candidacy proved stillborn. On one score, however, McGuinness could pass the reformers' purity tests. He was, by all standard measures, honest. "They'll never show anyone," he said time after time, "where Peter McGuinness ever stole a single vote or took a nickel for getting a pal a job."

In 1947, he was shocked and saddened by the death of his old friend Mayor LaGuardia. They had known each other almost three decades and there was a sincere friendship between the two men that transcended religious and political differences. He was in the hospital himself with a heart attack when he learned of the Little Flower's passing. His doctor's advised him not to attend, but McGuinness ignored their warnings and went anyway. He said, "No matter how much rain fell, I'd be there to pay him my respects. He was a corker of a little fellow." McGuinness recounted to a *Daily Eagle* journalist that once LaGuardia had offered him a job as city commissioner, even though McGuinness was not a Republican, and Peter told LaGuardia, "I am a Democratic leader of course and I cannot take it." McGuinness said, but LaGuardia replied: "Go on and take it; being without a job would never feed anyone." McGuinness would soon follow his old friend to the grave.

Chapter Twenty-Nine: Death and Legacy

June 14, 1948 was the saddest day in Greenpoint history—the day of McGuinness' funeral. The area was in deep shock and there was a neighborhood-wide sense of disbelief. Greenpoint's "First Citizen," its beloved boss, had passed, and no one could quite fathom how a man who had been so full of life, so joyful and exuberant, could be dead at such a young age. McGuinness was dead just short of his sixtieth year, yet no one could really quite grasp that his passing.

Of course, Mayor O'Dwyer, Borough President Cashman and all the other district leaders were there, but it was the reaction of the ordinary neighborhood people, not the dignitaries, that made the day so memorable. Ten thousand or more of Greenpoint's ordinary folk came onto the streets to say goodbye to their leader. No one could ever remember a larger outpouring of grief, nor a bigger Greenpoint funeral. A few old timers compared it with the 1909 death of local boss State Senator Patrick McCarren, but they quickly added that McGuinness was more loved and the people's grief was deeper and more sincere.

McGuinness was more than just a local power broker. His death was as if a close family member had passed. Somehow he had so come to embody the place that it was hard to think of Greenpoint without thinking of McGuinness and vice versa. The man and the place were synonymous with each other. McGuiness was, in fact, even more than a Greenpoint icon: he was the very personification of the working-class area. It was as if the community had suddenly lost its essence, and for thousands of locals the place would never really be the same again.

In the day since his passing, McGuinness was the constant topic of local conversation. Common people spoke of the many good deeds that Pete had done for his people and told countless stories of how Pete had gotten them jobs and how the food his club gave out at Christmas had kept them from hunger. People recalled how his humor and joy had lifted their spirits, especially in the dark moments of the depression.

The day of his funeral was more than just a black day —it was the end of an era. McGuinness, the benevolent Czar, was dead and his benevolent dictatorship had died with him. To many Greenpointers, his name was synonymous with statesmanship and now that statesman had passed on. Everyone sensed that no one would ever, or could ever, fully replace him. Many Greenpointers had grown up with little understanding of what government was about other than knowing Pete. *The Weekly Star*, told the story of the schoolboy or first-time voter asked to name the mayor, the governor, or the president who answered "Peter J. McGuinness" or "The McGuinness."

Much of the grief stemmed from the truth that McGuinness had loved Greenpoint's people as much as they had loved him. He once said, "I am very grateful to the people of the Garden Spot. They have been so kind and generous to me that I don't know the words to thank them. Not once have they let me down." Shortly before his death, he also said, "I have always tried to the best of my abilities to reflect credit both to the office and the trust of my neighbors and friends." He once put into words his love of his area, "There is no place on God's green earth like the Garden Spot of the world and among all the people of the world there are no finer ones than our right here in Greenpoint." After his heart attack and two days before his death, he gave a final message to his son for his constituents: "I love the people of Greenpoint and I am thankful for their support. My political success is due to their loyalty."

Of course, Greenpointers should have seen Pete's death coming. The year before he had taken a heart attack, but of course Pete brushed it off. He loved to eat, and despite losing weight he was still dangerously overweight, but no one thought he would die so prematurely. He was stricken with another attack and was taken to the hospital. Pete hung on for a few days in the hospital and there were even misleading reports of a recovery, then the awful news hit.

The funeral of course was the headline story in *The Brooklyn Daily Eagle*, and its cover picture showed crowds of distraught mourners dressed in black and wearing expressions of bewilderment. The service was also covered in all the local papers, including *The New York Times*, which wrote in his obituary, "He spent his life proving politicians could be colorful and honest."

Even *Time Magazine* covered the story and its correspondent perfectly captured the mood in the area, noting that locals never really thought Peter J. McGuinness would ever die. Time also noted that Pete was an old-fashioned Irish ward boss flourishing improbably in the 20th Century who falsely seemed as durable as the last of the cigar-store Indians. The *Time* correspondent observed that Pete was always in such demand as a pallbearer that it was almost impossible to imagine him playing a passive role at a funeral. *Time* summed up its coverage saying the obvious: "He was simply 'Greenpernt' to the rest of the world."

The crowds that came to the Edward Dowling Funeral Home on Norman Avenue for his wake were too large to accommodate everyone who wanted to pay their respects. Three hundred people stood outside the home the morning of the funeral simply to get a glimpse of the hearse as it left the home for the funeral mass.

The *Eagle* reported that ten thousand people lined the streets of Greenpoint and that people were six deep along Manhattan Avenue. All of the local businesses were closed as a sign of respect and many of the houses were draped in black. Because Pete's funeral was on Flag Day there seemed to be a sea of banners at half-mast.

There was a special detachment of twenty-five cops from the local precinct, but they had little to do, except to watch the thousands of numbed mourners on the sidewalks. The hearse reached stately St. Anthony's just before eleven for the funeral mass. More than three hundred people who were members of his political club, the Greenpoint People's Regular Democratic Club, preceded the coffin and filed into the church as a unit.

There were fifteen celebrants on the alter and the

church was jammed to capacity with hundreds of mourners. The Reverend Ambrose McGowan, who noted in his homily that Pete was a lifelong parishioner and that his father and uncles had been instrumental in building the church, sang the solemn high mass in Latin. Then, the service ended and the pallbearers lifted Pete's mahogany coffin. His pallbearers included the borough president, former judges, city aldermen, notable local politicians and businessmen.

They slowly carried the mahogany coffin to the hearse. An absolutely eerie, deathly silence pervaded the area broken only by the thud of the pallbearer's feet on the pavement. The coffin was placed in the hearse. The lead car carried Pete's widow and son. Fifty-five other cars followed as part of the procession, including five that just carried the mountain of flowers.

As his hearse slowly wended its way through the streets, the crowds were five and six deep. Hundreds of people on the streets burst into tears and thousands of men doffed their hats as the hearse passed. The hearse made a detour to pass the places of importance in his life. It rolled past his modest family home on Leonard Street and all its residents came out to the sidewalk to give one last good bye to the man with the big laugh. It passed his Greenpoint Regular People's Democratic Club on Norman Avenue where Pete had held forth like a Roman emperor. Finally, it left the area, taking McGuinness on his final journey to St. John's Cemetery in Queens.

His reputation for honesty followed him into death. He left only a small inheritance to his wife-proof that he never accepted graft. Today, it is unimaginable that a powerful leader would not end-up wealthy, but McGuinness died as he had lived—a man of modest means.

He was gone, but not forgotten. In life, McGuinness had set aside political differences to befriend Republicans and work with them. Thus, it was entirely in keeping with the bipartisan spirit of McGuinness that Salvatore Tortorici, a Greenpoint Republican, pressed local Alderman Joseph Sharkey in 1964 to sponsor a bill to rename Oakland Street, where McGuinness had once lived McGuinness Boulevard. The City Council passed the name change unanimously.

McGuinness was no angel, and he had flaws. His prejudice against Asians and Gypsies would be intolerable in a modern world that rejects all forms of bigotry and racism, but he had a genuine concern for the people and he worked tirelessly to make their lives better.

Today, there remain few people in their eighties and nineties who still remember McGuinness. Their faces light up with smiles when they pronounce his name. The local senior citizen center is named for him, but even there, many are too young to recall the greatest character in local history, but the bridges, pools, parks and other civic improvements he obtained for the area still remain and stand witness to his ability to deliver for Greenpoint. However, his greatest achievement was showing people that an ordinary honest man could make a profound difference and that people did not need to tolerate political corruption and stagnation. His life and career bear witness to the fact that people can still make democracy work effectively.

Epilogue

The McGuinness family abandoned the tiny frame house at 132 Eagle Street where Peter was born. A group of Polish men bought it and turned it into a social club called the St. Francis Club. They used the house for card games and drinking sessions, but as they matured and raised families they had little time to spend at the house, which quickly became run down and was soon empty.

In 1967, two Greenpoint youthful offenders were about to be released by New York State, but they had no place to live. Fr. Benedict Groeschel, a Franciscan Friar, the Chaplin at Children's Village in Dobbs Ferry, New York, wanted to find some kind of local lodging for the boys. He came across the St. Francis Club, then an abandoned house, and went to the Rectory of St Cyril Methodius Church to inquire about it. After hearing Fr. Benedict's need for the house, the club members signed the house over to him. Fr. Benedict's cousin made repairs to the house, getting it ready for habitation. It was renamed "the St. Francis House for Young Men" and the boys became its first residents.

The house, though, seemed to be haunted, and the new occupants were scared. Regularly they heard someone walking around upstairs. The lights inexplicably went on and off by themselves and other spooky things kept happening. Fr. Groeschel came to the house and witnessed the eerie actions himself. He immediately said mass for the ghost, whom he called McGuinness, after Peter McGuinness. He told the boys not to fear the ghost because it could not hurt them. Fr. Benedict spoke to the spirit and told McGuinness that if he was going to be in the house, he had a duty to protect the boys and the home. McGuinness hasn't turned a light on or off in many years, and he hasn't been heard upstairs walking around ever since.

Fr. Groeschel died, but the St. Francis House for Young Men has helped dozens of young men get a firm footing in life, and the house still continues as a refuge for troubled young men. All his life Peter was a charitable man who had a great love for children. McGuinness' spirit looks down from heaven on his house with an approving smile.

Bibliography

Chapter One: Manhattan Avenue March 10, 1927

Rovere, Richard THE BIG HELLO–I ***The New Yorker***, January 12, 1946

Page 29 Material on McGuinness' boxing career from Peter J. McGuinness by Boniface Fugelsang 1964 Master's Thesis St. Joseph's College.

Chapter Two: The Greenpoint People's Regular Democratic Club; Material came from Rovere and Pringle, Henry: The Gentleman from Greenpoint, *The American Mercury* April 1933

Chapter Three: March 11, 1927 Police Headquarters: *Night-Stick; The Autobiography of Lewis J. Valentine.* Main Author: Valentine, Lewis Joseph, 1882-1946. Language(s): English. Published: New York, Dial Press. 1944

Chapters Four: The Raid and five: The Aftermath *New York Times* March 13, 1927, *The Brooklyn Daily Eagle,* March 13th page 1 and March 19th 1927 page 1; Mitang, Herbert: *The Man who Rode the Tiger,* Fordham university Press 1996

Chapters Six: Early History and seven; McGuinness rewrites History McGuinness comments on the Monitor *New York Times* March 10, 1937 page 16 ; McGuinness arguments about Brooklyn history are in *The Brooklyn Daily Eagle* April 16, 1936 page 7

Chapter Eight: McGuinness' comments on his speech *Brooklyn Daily Eagle* article March 15, 1936; Zioncheck quote *Brooklyn Daily Eagle* May 30, 1936 page 11

Chapter Nine: Danger Town material on Danger Town *Greenpoint Brooklyn's Forgotten Past* Cobb, Geoffrey, North Brooklyn Neighborhood History May 2015, *Brooklyn Daily Eagle* July 18, 1886 page 3

Chapter Ten: McCarren's Machine; Material comes from *A Tree Grows in Brooklyn* by Betty Smith, Rovere and Flugelsang.

Chapter Eleven: The Fourteen McGuinnesses Rovere, Fugelsang and material about MacCrate friendship December 28, 1939 *Brooklyn Daily Eagle* article.

Chapter Twelve: The Celebrities of Greenpoint; *Greenpoint Brooklyn's Forgotten Past.*

Chapter Thirteen: Rovere and for information on Big Tim Sullivan Welch, Richard: *King of the Bowery Big Tim Sullivan, Tammany Hall, and New York City from the Gilded Age to the Progressive Era* ,SUNY Press 2009 pages 29-44

Chapter Fourteen: Orr's Lumber Yard. Material comes from Rovere and Fugelsang

Chapter Fifteen: Native Borns: *Brooklyn Daily Eagle* March 20, 1928 page 7

Chapter Sixteen: information about McGuinness in World War I in Fugelsang

Chapter Seventeen: Political Stirrings Information about McGuinness start in politics comes from Rovere and Fugelsang

Chapter Eighteen: The Most Colorful Alderman Ever Material from Rovere and Fugelsang. Baseball game material from *New York Times* July 13, 1934 page 27

Chapter Nineteen: Fighting Social Change: Material on McGuinness' smoking ban and fight against prohibition in Rovere.

Chapter Twenty: The Feud: Material on the fight with McQuade comes from Fugelsang, Rovere and April 1, 1928 *Brooklyn Daily Eagle* article page 1

Chapter Twenty-One Legislative Triumphs; Material on Gardens and Ferry from Rovere. Information on driving out Chinese illegals April 12, 1922 *Brooklyn Daily Eagle* page one and *Brooklyn Standard Union*, February 12, 1923 page 2

Chapter Twenty-Two: The Greenpoint People's Regular Democratic Club. Material from Rovere and Hylan's Parade *Brooklyn Standard Union* September 4, 1925 page 7

Chapter Twenty-Three: The Great Depression and the New Deal; Material comes from Rovere. Roosevelt Letter to McGuinness appeared in *Brooklyn Daily Eagle* April 12, 1944

Chapter Twenty-Four: Doubts. The poems come from Volume ten of the Peter J. McGuinness collected papers at Brooklyn College. The Whalen Raid material comes from a *New York Times* article June 25, 1929 page 5

Chapter Twenty-Five: Vindication: Mitang and October 13, 1931 *New York Times* Article page 9

Chapter Twenty-Six: Celebrations: O'Loughlin Article on Subway parade comes from Volume eleven of Peter J. McGuinness collected papers at Brooklyn College. Logan celebration comes from *New York Times* article June 24, 1934, page 12 The McCarren Park Pool information comes from the *New York Times* August 1, 1936 page 3

Chapter Twenty-Seven: Civic Virtue: *Brooklyn Daily Eagle* article February 22, 1935 page 1

Chapter Twenty-Eight: Continuity and Change Material on McQuade's surrender and views on Fusion reforms in Rovere. The letter to Tim Sullivan is from the McGuinness papers at Brooklyn College volume 13

Chapter Twenty-Nine: Death and Legacy: *Brooklyn Daily Eagle* article June 15 1948. Deathbed quotes from McGuinness in *Greenpoint Weekly Star* June 2, 1964

Acknowledgments

There are many people I would like to thank who helped make this book possible. My wife Maryla Cobb has supported me in many ways. I would also like to thank Marianne LaBatto and the staff at the Brooklyn College Archives for the great help in researching the McGuinness papers as well as Patrick Gilmour, Jennifer Cooper, John Herrick and others who gave me important critical feedback. I am indebted to Lian Calvo Serrano and Michael Whalen for their efforts in editing and proofreading my work. I am also very grateful to Amy Fierro whose design on the cover shows her great skill as a graphic designer. I would also like to thank Jorge Cruz who did invaluable work in formatting the text and working with the images and making the book look so professional.

93924221R00161

Made in the USA
Columbia, SC
24 April 2018